PATTON'S PHOTOGRAPHS

Related titles from Potomac Books

Photo Fakery: The History and Techniques of Photographic Deception and Manipulation
By Dino A. Brugioni

Eisenhower: Soldier-Statesman of the American Century
By Douglas Kinnard

The Pattons: A Personal History of an American Family
By Robert H. Patton

Patton at Bay: The Lorraine Campaign, 1944
By John Nelson Rickard

Brassey's D-Day Encyclopedia: The Normandy Invasion A-Z
By Barrett Tillman

War Slang: American Fighting Words and Phrases Since the Civil War
By Paul Dickson

An AUSA Book

PATTON'S PHOTOGRAPHS

War As He Saw It

Kevin Hymel

Foreword by Martin Blumenson

Potomac Books, Inc.
Washington, D.C.

Library of Congress Cataloging-in-Publication Data

Patton, George S. (George Smith), 1885-1945.
    Patton's photographs : war as he saw it / [compiled by] Kevin Hymel.— 1st ed.
      p. cm.
    Includes bibliographical references and index.
    ISBN 1-57488-871-4 (hardcover : alk. paper) — ISBN 1-57488-872-2 (pbk. : alk. paper)
      1. World War, 1939-1945—Campaigns—Pictorial works. 2. United States. Army—History—World War, 1939-1945—Pictorial works. 3. Soldiers—United States—History—20th century—Pictorial works. 4. Patton, George S. (George Smith), 1885-1945—Photograph collections. 5. Patton, George S. (George Smith), 1885-1945. 6. Generals—United States—Biography. I. Hymel, Kevin, 1966- II. Title.
    D743.2.P37 2005
    940.54'1273'0222—dc22

                                 2005015231

ISBN 1-57488-871-4   (hardcover)
ISBN 1-57488-872-2   (paperback) (alk. paper)

Printed in Canada on acid-free paper that meets the American National Standards Institute Z39-48 Standard.

Potomac Books, Inc.
22841 Quicksilver Drive
Dulles, Virginia 20166

First Edition

10 9 8 7 6 5 4 3 2 1

For Carl and Martin, without whom this book
would have never gotten off the ground.

So as through a glass, and darkly
The age-old strife I see
Where I fought under many guises
Many names—but always me.

—GEORGE S. PATTON, JR.

CONTENTS

ABOUT THE BOOK

The photographs that General Patton took were done with a simple camera during war. In this book, they are presented as close to their original form as possible. They were found in the general's albums and were meant as mementos and reminders of his travels. They are presented here in the same spirit.

FOREWORD

In a memorial service for George Smith Patton Jr. several days after his death, the Right Reverend W. Bertrand Stevens stated a profound truth about the general. Speaking at the Church of Our Savior in San Gabriel, California, where Patton had worshipped and where his parents were buried, the bishop said, "General Patton's life had a fullness and richness that is denied to most of us. . . . The variety of things he did in his lifetime . . . staggers the imagination."

The variety of things comprises a virtually boundless list of pursuits and interests. Patton was intensely curious, and he invited and entered into diverse experiences. For example, as he worked the pits on the firing range, he suddenly stood erect in a hail of bullets to put himself at risk and to judge whether he had overcome the emotion of fear. He also tinkered with practical matters, among them a sled he invented to carry the necessities of soldiers in the attack.

Horses were a distinct part of his existence, and from an early age, Patton loved them, rode them, raced them. A master of equitation, he steeplechased, showed and jumped them. He played polo on their backs and dashed through the fields with them in chase of the fox. Vocationally, he was a cavalryman, and he enjoyed the ceremonial parade as well as the stirring charge.

As a boy, Patton was an expert marksman with the rifle, and he hunted wild goats on Santa Catalina Island. He swam and fished and sailed in the island's waters. Later in life, after studying the art of navigation, he took his yacht from the coast of California to Hawaii and back.

Wondering what made motorcars run, Patton took the engine of his automobile apart and put it back together. His knowledge of mechanics helped turn him to the tanks in World War I. He learned how they worked and were kept in repair, and how the

French and British trained tankers and employed them in battle. He penned lengthy memos defining the tank's structure and capabilities, the organization of tank units, the tactics of tank forces, and the methods of instruction and drill. He headed a school for tankers, then led them in combat to great triumph. He was the foremost American tanker of that time.

Patton fired the pistol with authority. On the frontier in Texas where cowboys and outlaws abounded, he made what he called "the darndest shot you ever saw." While riding a horse at the trot, he hit a jackrabbit running about fifteen feet away. Marveling in surprise, he informed his wife, "My reputation as a gunman is made."

He participated in the 1912 Olympic Games held in Stockholm and competed in the Modern Pentathlon—pistol shooting, swimming, fencing, riding, and the steeplechase. The event tested the fitness of the man at arms, and Patton made a good showing. He had learned to use the broadsword at West Point, and after the Olympics he took lessons at the French cavalry school. He was so good that the Army appointed him, when he was still a young lieutenant, Master of the Sword. He was the first to hold the exalted title. He then taught fencing at Fort Riley. He also designed and oversaw the mass production of a new weapon known as the Patton saber.

The general conceived and modeled a special uniform for his tankers. Of dark green gabardine, a color concealing grease spots, the suit consisted of a jacket with a row of white or brass buttons down the sides and trousers padded to cushion the shocks of travel, with pockets on the legs for first aid items, maps, and ammunition. Headgear resembled a football helmet. The ensemble was comic in appearance. Even Patton had to admit that regulation issue was better clothing. But he had had great fun devising and wearing his creation.

He became an airplane pilot to see for himself how enemy fliers observed military forces on the ground. He did so in order to seek solutions for his units to evade harassment from the air. In a letter to a friend, he promised to take him for a ride "if you have sufficient insurance."

"This picturesque and dashing officer," the *Washington Sunday Star* said in December 1940, "can do a multitude of things."

He wrote scads of poetry, martial verse for the most part, sixteen articles published in professional journals, and two book-length manuscripts. He liked to sing, and his rendition of "Lily from Piccadilly" was classic. His wife, who composed a march for his armored division, thought he should play a musical instrument and bought him a saxophone; if he tootled, it was not for long.

During World War II, he was an amateur photographer. Taking pictures gave him great pleasure. The snapshots preserved the personal record of the places he passed through during the conflict. They reported on what he deemed to be interesting or important.

Kevin Hymel, a military historian whose expertise encompasses the twentieth century, has collected, chosen, and captioned the best of General Patton's photographs with great sensitivity and skill. His remarks are clear, direct, and to the point, for he knows a great deal about the commander and his campaigns. The pictures, snapped as you or I might have done, together with Kevin Hymel's interpretation, give insight into Patton's personality and character. They present another facet of Patton's complex being. Without destroying the general's legend, Mr. Hymel has made him immensely human.

MARTIN BLUMENSON

PREFACE

In 1996 I made an amazing discovery. I was researching Gen. George S. Patton at the Library of Congress when I noticed something interesting in the Patton index: lists of photo albums. Curious, I requested a few volumes. They were huge, coffee-table-sized books. I opened one and realized I was looking at the actual pictures Patton took during World War II: black and white pictures of soldiers, tanks and ancient ruins. Mixed in were official Signal Corps photos and pictures of the general that others had taken. There were also extensive captions, notes and letters explaining things that were not with the usual collection. What a gold mine! I found myself ordering the entire collection and poring over the photographs for days.

I went through every Patton book I owned and found that none of these pictures had been accessed before. Eventually, I began checking the pictures against Patton's diaries and letters and found they were providing a whole new dimension on one of World War II's greatest commanders.

I wrote an article about my find and gave it to Martin Blumenson, the famed Patton author and historian, to edit. I had included a paragraph about how Martin became the official biographer of Patton and had edited the general's papers and photographs for publication. When he returned the article I asked him if he had learned anything new about Patton from it. "Yes," he said. "I didn't know Patton had a photo collection." Again, I was shocked at my discovery.

The project languished after awhile. I had submitted the article to a number of history magazines, including some I worked for as a photo and art coordinator. But, without the actual pictures, which I could not afford to copy, no one was interested.

Finally, in 2001, I pitched the idea to Carl Gnam, the publisher of *WWII History* Magazine. I had worked for Carl as an editor and was still working for him as his part-time photo and art director. Carl had a knack for knowing a winner. He liked the idea and agreed to pay for the photo development. I was on my way. With Carl's backing and Martin's mentoring, the picture essay made it into *WWII History* as the cover story, becoming the best selling issue of the magazine.

But a photo essay in a magazine could not do justice to fifteen photo albums of Patton pictures. While making a final review with Martin, the idea came to me that

the collection might make an interesting book. Martin's saying, "I'm excited about it," was all I needed to move forward.

I have done my best to present Patton's photos in chronological order, but few had dates and many were out of order in the albums, compared to what was explained in the General's diaries. Patton often sent bundles of pictures to his wife, leaving her to sort them out. When there was no information with a particular picture, I used Patton's own words to define the scene. Not all the pictures are here, either. I chose the ones most relevant to Patton's story and left out some of the more ordinary photos. I have tried to limit the use of Signal Corp photos and use only those to which Patton made specific reference.

I am indebted to Martin and Carl for their help. Carl was the spark while Martin provided guidance and advice throughout the writing process. Martin spent hours reviewing the text with me. Watching him hone my prose was like watching a surgeon perform a heart transplant. The man's knowledge of Patton and World War II knew no bounds.

The staff at the Library of Congress, Manuscripts Division was also helpful, friendly and enthusiastic about my project. Daun van Ee, the Historical Specialist, gave me permission to copy the photos. Fred Bauman helped me with the bulky albums on the copying machine.

The people at Potomac Books, Inc., did a fantastic job of putting up with a new author. Paul Merzlak, my initial contact at the company, kept me informed on the book's status. Jehanne Moharram cleaned up the text and helped me add sidebars that I thought fleshed out the subject better. John Church and Michie Shaw put the book together and improved the pictures. Claire Noble responded to all my requests for more promotion flyers and listened to my other promotion ideas. And Rick Russell oversaw the whole process.

My father, Gary G. Hymel, an author in his own right, also read over my text and made suggestions. My friend and coworker Pete Murphy went above and beyond the call of duty to take pictures of Patton's camera at Fort Knox, Kentucky. My friend Paul Karpers made some very helpful suggestions on the Introduction. Andrew Gibson provided key wording and added flow. Michael Dolan, one of the best researchers I know, found audiotapes of Patton's speeches during his 1945 War Bond Drive. Ron

Covill, at the Association of the United States Army, upgraded my computer numerous times. Merry Pantano, my agent, guided me through the book making process and pushed me when I needed to be pushed. Bob Knudsen photographed all of Patton's pictures at the Library of Congress, saving me time and money. Danielle Giovannelli edited my text from the non-military reader's point of view. Samantha Detuello laid out the first two chapters so I could see how my ideas translated onto the page. Chris and Anna Anderson offered advice and inspiration when the project seemed overwhelming. Ed Mueller found my good side for the picture on the back flap. Dr. Jim Regan gave me hope when I could not find any.

All opinions and interpretations expressed in this book are mine alone and all errors, both of omission and commission, are my responsibility.

I
THE GENERAL AND HIS HOBBY

Patton. The name alone conjures images of a general sporting two ivory-handled pistols, a brilliant battlefield commander and tough-talking fighter. George S. Patton, Jr., was all of those things. He was also an amateur photographer. In combat or on a historical tour, he snapped away at anything that interested him in North Africa, Sicily and continental Europe.

Even under fire or in harsh elements, Patton could usually spot something worth his lens. He took pictures of almost everything, from combat to ancient ruins. He used his camera to explain people he met, record advancements in enemy technology and assist himself in understanding his fighting arenas. He also simply took pictures of his daily surroundings.

For Patton, history was everything. Be it a Roman ruin or the history he was making, he wanted a record kept, both for personal use and for historians. Diaries and letters were not enough. Only by carrying his camera into battle could he ensure an accurate depiction of events, free from interpretation.

Patton's picture-taking added to his colorful legend. In Italy, he claimed his hobby prevented his death. Touring the front, he stopped to take a picture. A salvo of German shells exploded up the road ahead. The photograph, he wrote, "saved my life."

Patton's Leica camera, shown front and back, is held at the Patton Museum of Cavalry and Armor at Fort Knox, Kentucky.

Toward the end of the war, when a Spitfire pilot mistook Patton's Piper Cub for a German Storch and strafed it three times over Germany, Patton took out his camera and photographed the action. Unfortunately, he left the lens cap on.[1]

His staff officers were frequently in his lens, not as subjects of a picture, but to give size and dimension to enemy tanks, shell craters or Greek columns. His dog Willie, on the other hand, was a star in his own right.

Although Patton had more than one camera, his favorite one was his German-made, 35mm Leica. It was covered with black leatherette with a label on the back, which he wore down from constant use. It was a common camera, issued to

reporters and historians in the American army. Patton's camera case, however, was emblazoned with the gold initials "G.S.P., Jr." on the back.[2]

As he took more and more pictures, Patton sent them to his wife, Beatrice. He sent bundles to be sorted out and catalogued. Included with his own pictures were U.S. Army Signal Corps photos and pictures of himself taken by others. Patton could be a real taskmaster, often suggesting where she could get duplicates made and constantly asking her if she had received the latest batch.

In fact, the story of Patton's picture-taking is the story about the general and his wife. In many of his letters, Patton reserved a few words for his photography. He explained the pictures enclosed and pictures that were to come. He also requested film and new cameras from her. Beatrice became the depository of her husband's collection, and fixing the photographs into albums became an almost full-time job. If her husband wrote on the back of a picture, she transcribed it onto the album page. It was no easy task. Patton would send photos months after taking them, leaving her to sort them out. One picture he took in June, before D-Day, he sent to her in September, three months later.[3] His collection eventually filled fifteen albums. Patton's pictures show the victorious face of war: American GIs on the move, military bridges under construction and Sherman tanks with hedgerow cutters welded to their hulls, slicing through the Normandy countryside. They also show defeat: smashed German tanks, hapless

prisoners of war, and dead enemy bodies strewn across the landscape. Along with pictures of modern war, Patton took shots of historic sights and of the different terrain in North Africa and Europe.

Patton's photography reflects the experience most professional photographers had in World War II. Like the pros, his early photographs are mostly posed pictures of acquaintances or still lifes of equipment far behind the lines or destroyed vehicles the war had passed by. As the war endured, the pictures got closer and closer to the action; nameless front-line soldiers, enemy bodies and destroyed vehicles still smoking from recent battles filled the lens.

Although World War II was well covered by photographers, these pictures are from Patton's eye. Imagine if George Washington, Ulysses S. Grant or Robert E. Lee had had a camera with them during their campaigns. How valuable would those pictures be? Historians and biographers spend years poring over diaries, letters, and notes of their subjects, trying to get inside their heads. What could be more valuable than actually seeing the things an historical figure thought were important enough to record on film? What could be more revealing?

To Patton, getting the story right was everything. Indeed, in one of his first letters to his wife after arriving in North Africa, he mentioned sending her a trove of his files for the express reason to "help some future historian to write a less untrue history than usual."[4]

The collection is impressive and helps explain America's foremost combat commander in World War II. If Patton truly relished the glory of war, the excitement of the fight, then these pictures reinforce his beliefs and add to his legend.

II
NORTH AFRICA

World War II began for George S. Patton, Jr., on November 8, 1942, when his Western Task Force landed on the shores of Morocco in North Africa. He came ashore at Fedhala Beach near Casablanca, where he spent his time getting his soldiers ashore, leaving no time for picture taking.

Patton's Western Task Force was one of three landings in Operation Torch, a combined British and American amphibious offensive designed to get Allied forces into North Africa. Despite the lack of training and inexperience, and being cooped up in ships for weeks, the Western Task Force came safely ashore and Patton began organizing his forces to assault Casablanca. But before he could attack, the French commander, Gen. Auguste P. Nogues, surrendered the city and the American army marched in peacefully. Patton's landing was a success.[1]

In one of Patton's first letters from Africa to his wife, Beatrice, he told her he would soon be sending letters and rolls of film from his time on board the USS *Augusta*, his cruiser headquarters.[2] Almost every following letter to Bea contained a reference to his photography, either explaining the pictures he sent —". . . and you can have enlargements made of those you want,"— or instructing her to buy more film.[3]

His battlefield responsibilities over, Patton took over as the military governor of Morocco. He went from directing troops and overseeing logistics to spending his days visiting dignitaries, attending parades, touring cities, and hunting wild boar, taking pictures throughout. He was responsible for billeting and security at the Casablanca conference, where President Franklin D. Roosevelt, Prime Minister Winston Churchill, and their advisors met to settle the direction of the war.

Patton took pictures from the dramatic—views from the nose of a bomber—to the mundane—"I just took a picture of my desk which I will send as soon as the rest of the rol [sic] is completed." To improve on his photography, he even had his ordnance department develop a quick rewind device for his camera.[4] The camera also helped him satisfy his interest in ancient history. On trips across Morocco and Tunisia, he would order his driver to stop so he could take snapshots of the relics of antiquity. "The Roman ruins are wonderful and all over," he wrote. "One gets quite used to passing huge cities and not even knowing their names."[5]

Although he posed for many pictures, he was not impressed with his own looks. When photographers caught him exiting a movie theater, he confessed: "I do not photograph well, or I think I look better than I do—probably the latter."

Patton's war begins, as he heads off to the North African shore. His clothes were yellowed from a French dye marker which splashed near him during the sea battle with the Vichy. He captioned this picture, "Three cheers for Gen. Patton."[6]

Events in Tunisia eventually pulled Patton out of his political position and back to battlefield command. Erwin Rommel's Africa Korps had smashed into the American II Corps, rolling it back fifty miles to the Kasserine Pass. Patton was called in to take over, restore morale, fire ineffective officers, and get the II Corps back into the fight. He was also promoted to lieutenant general.

On March 6, Patton took command and began whipping the II Corps into shape. Within ten days he had the Americans on the offensive. When the German 10th

PATTON'S TEAM

Patton brought with him to North Africa a team of trusted advisors, commanders and soldiers. Some would be with him for the rest of the war, a few would go on to command units in other theaters, and one would succumb to the harsh fighting in the desert.[7]

Maj. Gen. Geoffrey Keys, Deputy Commanding General

Lt. Al Stiller, Aide de Camp

Col. Hobart Gay, Chief of Staff

S.Sgt. George Meeks, Patton's orderly

Admiral H. Kent Hewitt, naval commander of the Western Task Force

Capt. Richard M. Jensen, Aide de Camp

Panzer Division attacked at El Guettar, Patton stopped the Germans cold, handing the Axis their first defeat at American hands.

The U.S. troops at Maknassy did not fare as well, and Patton relieved the division commander. Keeping the II Corps on the offensive was Patton's main concern. He

The arrow, drawn by Patton, shows the spot on Fedhala Beach where he landed. He credited the smooth landing of his troops to the calm tides that prevailed, despite predictions that the surf would be rough; to Patton this was a sign of divine providence.[8]

The next day Patton was on the beach when French planes strafed the area. When a soldier panicked and ran from his post, Patton "kicked him in the arse with all my might," and the soldier returned to duty. Ever the self-promoter, Patton attached a note to this picture, telling his wife that it would make a good magazine cover.[9]

Patton's Beatrice

She was there for it all: The West Point years, the Pancho Villa expedition, World War I, the lull that followed and, of course, World War II. She may not have been at her husband's elbow as he made history, but she was always connected to him by letters and pictures.

Beatrice Ayer Patton was a feisty, beautiful woman who drew people to her, helping her husband's career through her popularity; everyone wanted the charming woman at their social gatherings. But she was not only pretty, she spoke French, German, Italian, Spanish, and a little Hawaiian. For sports, she enjoyed fox hunting, sailing and deep sea fishing. She also dabbled in poetry like her husband and enjoyed writing fiction.[1]

She first met George S. Patton Jr. when they were teenagers on Catalina Island in California in the summer of 1902. Their families got together to vacation, put on plays and argue politics. At first, George was not drawn to the girl from Boston, Massachusetts, but he eventually came around and they developed a correspondence from opposite sides of the continent. It was good practice for the future when they would be twice separated by an ocean.

As their relationship grew, they visited whenever they could. At West Point, George invited her to dances and weekend visits. He proposed to her as he was graduating; her father, however, was against it, believing his daughter should not marry an army officer. But George persisted, and Beatrice's hunger strike certainly helped. Her father eventually relented and the two wed on May 26, 1910, in Avalon, Massachusetts.

They honeymooned in England, where Bea became pregnant. She soon bore a daughter, whom they christened "Little Bee." Little Bee got a sister in 1915 when Ruth Ellen was born. It would not be until 1923 that Bea would give birth to a son, George IV. At first army life was not easy for Bea. Frontier posts held few creature comforts and lacked the cultural activities of the east coast. When George went to Mexico to pursue Pancho Villa and later to France during the First World War, she returned to Massachusetts.

She was with him for his state-side posts and sailed with him to Stockholm, Sweden, when he competed in the modern pentathlon in the 1912 Olympics. She encouraged him while he trained and cheered him while he ran, shot, dueled, rode, and swam. When he failed to win the pistol match, Beatrice blamed herself for keeping him out too late the night before at a party.[2]

George returned from the battlefields of France in 1919 and, like many veterans, reacquainted himself with his wife. They moved to Fort Meade, Maryland, where Bea befriended the wife of another officer, Dwight D. Eisenhower. She cooked for Ike's wife, Mamie, who did not know her way around a kitchen. Later, the family embarked for a tour of duty in Hawaii, where Bea immersed herself in Hawaiian history and lore. When George was stationed at Fort Myers, Virginia, the Bonus Marchers came to Washington, D.C., and Bea took her children to meet Joe Angelo, the man who had saved George's life during World War I and had him retell the tale to her children, proving what a hero her husband was.

She was a very attentive mother. Much like her husband, she gave her daughters maxims to live by: "When in doubt about what to do, the kind thing is usually the right thing;" "A gentleman is one who never hurts anyone's feelings by mistake"; and "A lady is a woman who behaves like a gentleman." But she could be short with them. When Little Bee announced her engagement Beatrice slapped her,

(Continued)

BEATRICE *(CONTINUED)*

shouting that she was too young to marry. Bee was not too young; Beatrice and George were just getting older but they did not want to admit it.

When it came time for a second tour in Hawaii, George was in a bad mood. Feeling like his career had stalled, he decided to boost his sagging ego by sailing to the islands in a fifty-two-foot schooner. Beatrice insisted that she come along as cook. She came into her own in Hawaii, where her interests in archeology, anthropology, history and local lore converged as she visited caves, attended luaus and learned Hawaiian curses. Inspired by what she learned, she wrote *Blood of the Shark,* a romance novel that took place in 1793 Hawaii. George was terribly unsupportive. He not only discouraged her efforts, he had an affair with Jean Gordon, Beatrice's twenty-one-year-old half niece. When Jean left the islands to complete her tour of the Far East, Beatrice thought about ending the marriage but finally decided that "he needs me more than I need him." They rekindled their marriage.

During World War II, Beatrice was busier than ever. She gave radio addresses, wrote patriotic stories, attended luncheons and fundraisers, and, of course, constantly corresponded with her husband and organized his pictures. She kept scrapbooks of his activities until the slapping incident in Sicily. The stories on the incident shocked her and she accused the reporters of having "no shame." Ruth Ellen took over the scrap books after that. Beatrice also hardly ever used her car, worried that she was depriving her husband's tanks of gasoline. Instead she rode a donkey cart to church or into town.[3]

She kept up with George's correspondence, reinforcing his ego and defending him against detractors. She kept him up to date on their children and friends and let him know what was being said about him in the hometown newspapers. But it was not all an information exchange. They both spoke

of how much they missed each other and she even encouraged him to smile more often for the cameras, reminding him that "forty centuries are looking at you." [4]

When he returned from the war almost three years later, they had little time alone, touring the country on a war bonds drive. When it was over he flew back to Germany. He planned to return to her and retire, but somehow he knew he would never come back. When George had his accident in Germany, she flew there with the country's best spinal cord doctor and an Army escort. She sat between the pilots on a rigged swing, entertaining them the whole way. She was at George's side as he deteriorated and remained in Europe for the funeral in Hamm, Luxembourg.[5]

After the war she worked to keep her husband's legacy alive, attending numerous statue, memorial, and museum dedications for her Georgie. She had his diaries and letters, with their scribble-style that George wrote in, transcribed and annotated. She compiled his World War II diary entries into a book, *War As I Knew It,* which was published in 1947. She also arranged a meeting with Jean Gordon, her husband's mistress, and put a Hawaiian curse on her; a few weeks later Jean was dead by her own hand.[6]

On September 30, 1956, at the age of 67, Beatrice took a fall from a horse; she did not get up. She had suffered an aortic aneurism burst, a condition she had kept secret. She wanted to be buried with her husband, but only soldiers were buried at military cemeteries in Europe. Instead, she was cremated and her urn was buried on her property for several years until her two surviving children flew to Hamm and sprinkled her ashes over George's grave. They were finally together in peace. ●

(Continued from page 8)

sent Col. Clarence C. Benson forward to punch through the German lines with an armored thrust. Patton accompanied Benson to the front and took pictures while artillery rained down around them.[10] However slowly, the Americans kept on the offensive. Patton proved his leadership.

But success came at a personal price. On April 1, Patton's aide, Capt. Richard M. Jensen, whose family Patton knew while growing up in California, was killed in a German bombing attack. Patton, overwhelmed with grief, visited the grave, where he took pictures.

The war in North Africa ended for Patton with more of a whimper than a bang. Slated to command the American forces in the invasion of Sicily, he gave the reins of II Corps to Maj. Gen. Omar Bradley and began training units that would eventually make up the Seventh Army.[11] During the preparations for invasion, he wrote Bea about one of his biggest problems: "I am having trouble with my 35-Eastman Kodak," and asked her to send him a Leica camera. He hoped to take color pictures.[12]

THE BATTLE FOR PORT LYAUTEY

The toughest French resistance against Patton came from a castle named the Kasbah at Port Lyautey, an inland town along a bend in the Sebou River. For three days, Patton's troops attacked the castle only to be repulsed or face small attacks spearheaded by French World War I tanks. It was not until two howitzers brought the castle under fire and Navy dive-bombers attacked that the French surrendered.

The Kasbah was defended by approximately 200 French soldiers.

The wall and ditch forced the Americans to attack the castle's gate.

A howitzer breached the wall of the Kasbah here. Patton wrote that the men then charged through "with bayonets and hand grenades in true movie style."

The castle gate was opened for good after the Americans stormed the fort.

The battle's first casualty. Lt. Col. Demas T. Craw approached the Kasbah with a white flag and was killed by enemy machine gun fire. He was posthumously awarded the Medal of Honor for his actions.

(Above) Some of Patton's troops landed at Safi, about 150 miles south of Morocco. The assault on this French garrison was so quick and so efficient that the Americans lost only four soldiers.

(Right) Sunken ships line the waterfront in Casablanca.

The prize of Torch: on November 11—three days after the invasion— American soldiers enter Casablanca on Patton's birthday. "I said I would take Casa by D plus 3," he confided to his diary, "and I did. A nice birthday present." [13]

Once the fighting stopped, Patton met with French Gen. Auguste Nogues and Adm. François Michelier to accept their surrender. Here, Patton examines an American 16-inch shell that landed in Gen. Nogues' dining room. Behind Patton is Adm. Michelier, whose naval forces attacked the American fleet during the Torch landings. Patton was particularly impressed with the admiral. "He fought to the last and is now a great friend. He is a man." [14]

Anti-aircraft fire lights up the night sky around Casablanca.

FIRST MEETING WITH THE SULTAN

Shortly after the successful Torch landings, Patton met with Sultan Mohammad V of Morocco. He was impressed with what he saw, particularly the "inner court filled with white robed men in biblical dress. The visit was short, with Patton guaranteeing his American forces would respect the country's "Mohammedan" institutions. Patton would visit the Sultan often after that, attending ceremonies, delivering letters from President Roosevelt and representing the United States to its new ally.

(Left) Patton heads into the Sultan's quarters.

(Below) Patton presents himself before the Sultan.

The Sultan's advisors. On the other side of the lattice wall was the Sultan's harem. Patton himself peeked through the screen to notice a number of the women wore glasses.

—— THE AMERICAN PASHA ——

Once Patton captured all his objectives in the Torch landings, he took over as the military head of Morocco. He basically ruled the western third of North Africa, deciding on tasks military and civilian, making sure supplies moved off the docks and into American hands, and keeping the peace between the Arabs and the French, while taking the occasional boar hunt or fishing trip. He hated every second of it.

Patton did not want to work in an administrative position while there was fighting going on, but this was where the war effort needed him, at least temporarily. He spent most of his time in meetings either with Allied leaders or with the Sultan of Morocco. He would also head down to the docks to watch unloading operations or visit regimental camps. The only excitement came from an occasional nighttime air attack by Axis planes.

His most time-consuming duty was constantly pacifying the French, who were worried about their authority over the Arabs, and the Arabs, who were terrified of a Jewish uprising backed by the Ameri-

can army. The Sultan would call for Patton and monopolize him for hours about these worries, usually over elaborate meals. To ease the Sultan's mind Patton always responded to the requests and made sure there was an American military presence at ceremonies and parades. At one parade, Patton noticed an Arab woman wave at him, which was against the law. "I hope Allah did not see her," he mused to his diary.

His outdoor excursions with the Sultan were not very exhaustive. They were elaborately planned and accompanied by servants and cooks. The hunts he went on employed 250 natives as beaters who went into the brush to flush animals into the path of the hunter. His fishing trips were the same, a caravan of vehicles or horses heading out to a well-established fishing spot.

All the while Patton worried about the American position in the war and saw other commanders advancing past him. On December 1 he was visiting with General Eisenhower and Lt. Gen. Mark Wayne Clark when Eisenhower took a phone

Patton rides his armored car with the Sultan of Morocco and his Grand Vizier (front seat) on an inspection tour of U.S. forces. Patton claimed to be the first foreigner to ever be allowed to ride with the Sultan.

call. When he hung up he said, "Well, Wayne, you get the Fifth Army." Patton was shocked, realizing that he would remain a corps commander. It bothered him so much he was unable to sleep that night. Later, when he learned about the troop distribution in North Africa that would have one American division fighting under a French corps, he railed that America had sold its birthright just to have an American named as Allied commander.

Patton jumped at any opportunity to get away from his desk and close to the front in Tunisia. He visited the troops, combat commanders, and, on occasion, spots where friends had been killed. One visit on December 9 especially worried him. During his flight to the front his plane was fired on by Allied anti-aircraft guns, tearing a hole in the wing. He then drove to the front, visiting various British and American command posts. It was during this drive that he came across his son-in-law, John Waters.

Patton did not like what he found at the front: drunken generals, poor tactical tank deployments, and front-line troops who told him he was the only general officer they had seen in almost a month. In addition, sheep herders seemed to be on every road, impeding the progress of supply convoys. He reported his findings directly to General Eisenhower.

The highlight of Patton's time between combat commands was the Casablanca Conference, where he got to meet with President Roosevelt, Winston Churchill and their staffs. He was offered two jobs during the conference: one from Eisenhower to be the deputy commander of American forces in North Africa, and one from Harry Hopkins, a presidential advisor, who offered Patton an ambassadorship. He was interested in neither.

Finally when the dust started to settle from the disaster at Kasserine Pass, Eisenhower called for Patton to take over II Corps. His long wait in the rear was over and he was back in the saddle of a battlefield command. ●

At times Patton's comments about civilians could be as audacious as the ones to his soldiers. Of this photo of local North African women he wrote, "The least bad-looking."[15] Women without veils were "unfortunate because it clearly destroys any illusions as to the beauty of Arabian women."[16]

The Sultan of Morocco presented Patton with this Grand Cross of the Order of Ouissam Alaouite, a sash with a medal at its end, and told him "the lions in the desert tremble at his approach." Patton proudly sent this picture to Beatrice with the quote written in French.

Patton poses for the camera after the presentation of the Order of Ouissam Alaouite. In the center, left to right, are the Grand Vizier, Gen. Nogues, the Sultan, the Prince Imperial, and Patton.

Patton, left, dressed in African robes with a solid gold scabbard, poses with the Sultan of Morocco and Gen. Nogues. Patton prided himself on his political dealings with the Arabs and French, boasting, "I should have been a statesman."[17]

(Below) Patton checks out a local market. "This is a great country for photography," he wrote to Beatrice, "as everything is queer. You meet camels, burros, horses, and Arabs on the same road with tanks and self-propelled artillery."[18]

PATTON'S CAPTURED SON-IN-LAW

In mid-December, Patton drove out into the desert to meet with his son-in-law, Lt. Col. John Waters, a battalion commander with the 1st Armored Division. These are the last pictures taken of Waters before his capture. After the battle, Patton visited the spot where he was captured and picked up two cartridge cases and two bullets and sent them to his daughter, Beatrice. Waters spent the rest of the war in a German POW camp.[19]

Col. John Waters, battalion commander with the 1st Armored Division and Patton's son-in-law. Patton noticed that Waters had a bullet hole in his coat.[20]

Back in the United States, John's Silver Star with Oak Leaf Cluster is pinned on his son, John Jr. Beatrice Waters and Mrs. Patton stand in the background.

Patton watches a troop of Spanish legionnaires pass in review in the Spanish-controlled part of Morocco. Patton considered them "the best looking infantry I have seen yet."

(Above) At the Casablanca Conference, the meeting between President Roosevelt and Prime Minister Churchill, and their advisors, Patton took pictures of the men, but lamented that the official photographs were taken "for the glory of F.D.R. and not the troops."[21]

(Right) Patton has lunch with President Roosevelt and Lt. Gen. Mark Clark during the Casablanca conference.

While military governor, Patton spent time hunting. On one excursion a boar charged him. Patton shot the animal in the right eye but its momentum carried it right to his feet, spilling blood on his boots. Patton claimed the boar, "My biggest pig." He strapped it onto the hood of his halftrack, with two others, for the trip back to his headquarters and sent the animal's teeth to Beatrice.[22]

The first picture of Patton with three stars. After the American disaster at Kasserine Pass, Patton was given command of II Corps and promoted to lieutenant general.

(Left) To celebrate his promotion, Patton posed for pictures, sporting a gold football helmet with three stars. "When I was a little boy at home," he confided to his diary, "I used to wear a wooden sword and say to myself, 'George S. Patton, Jr., Lieutenant General.' At that time I did not know there were full generals. Now I want and will get four stars."[23]

Patton's II Corps headquarters in Feriana.

As the commander of II Corps, Patton often stopped on his way to the front to photograph the German army's destruction. He took this picture at Sidi Bou Zid. His command car, with II Corps markings and two of his three stars visible, is in the foreground. "It was very realistic to pass burning trucks and smoldering tanks on the road, and to see the mine fields [sic] with the engineers removing mines," he wrote to his son.[24]

Two of Patton's best fighters were Terry Allen, the commander of the 1st Infantry Division (left) and Lt. Col. Orlando Darby of the U.S. Army Rangers. When later offered a promotion, Darby turned it down, preferring to stay with his men. "This is the first time I ever saw a man turn down a promotion," Patton mused. "He is a great soldier."

Patton wrote on the back of this picture, "This was all that was left of five Germans."[25]

Omar Bradley poses with Maj. Gen. Harold Bull and another officer. Bradley served as Patton's deputy commander at II Corps.

Patton was constantly at the front, overseeing the progress of II Corps, and, when time permitted, taking pictures of his staff. "I still get scared under fire," he confessed. "I guess I will never get used to it, but I still poke along. I dislike the strafing the most."[26]

To break through the German lines, Patton assigned Col. Clarence Benson to attack with armor. He was there for Benson's jump-off and took this picture of Benson in his command tank, the *Alamo*, as German artillery shells fell. "I got some pictures, but missed one fine salvo just in front of the hill I was sitting on."

ABOVE THE BATTLEFIELD

After the victory in North Africa, Patton took to the air to record the details of his success.[27]

German tanks attacked here on March 21. The impact of Allied air strikes dots the landscape.

By the time Patton took this picture of Tebessa, the American supply dumps, marked with "X's," were no longer visible from the sky. The arrow points to a forward observation post.

One of Patton's infantry regiments assaulted this ridge five times on April 5 without success until Patton got the "personal idea" to hit it with 25 rounds of white phosphorous and 25 rounds of high explosive artillery. The hill was taken without a loss. The previous attacks had lost 26 percent of the assaulting troops.

THE DEATH OF CAPTAIN JENSEN

When Capt. Richard Jensen was killed in a German dive-bomb attack, Patton was inconsolable. Patton knew Jensen's family while growing up in California and the General considered his young aide a man of "great character." Patton visited the spot where Jensen was killed, and later his grave a number of times. He took pictures for Jensen's parents.

Patton snapped this picture on the day Capt. Jensen was killed.

(Right) Just before battle, Jensen (with goggles on his helmet) discusses a plan of attack with other officers.

(Below) Lt. Alexander Stiller, one of Patton's aides, stands in the crater where Jensen was killed.[28]

Before leaving Tunisia, Patton visited Jensen's grave to pay his last respects, lay flowers, and take pictures of the mound. He placed the bouquet of nasturtiums, visible in this photograph, on the grave.[29]

As the II Corps continued to press the Germans, Patton visited the town of Timgambia, (today's Timgad), which was founded by the Roman emperor Trajan in AD 100. Patton, while impressed with the town, commented: "I have fought and won a bigger battle than Trajan ever heard of." He wrote on this photo, "Trajan's arch, old and new conqueror."[30]

In Algeria, Patton readies his troops for the invasion of Sicily. The training stressed fighting in close quarters for the anticipated house-to-house battles ahead.[31] To see how effective this street fighting scenario was, Patton went through it himself, with bullets passing overhead. "It frightened me to death," he admitted.[32]

III
SICILY

With North Africa safely in Allied hands, Patton next led the U.S. Seventh Army in the invasion of Sicily. He came ashore at the Gulf of Gela with his camera slung over one shoulder, freeing his neck for his binoculars. Soon he was in the thick of battle, directing the defense of his beachhead as the Axis counterattacked.

The Seventh Army was tasked with protecting the left flank of the British Eighth Army at Syracuse, and continuing that job until the British reached Messina, the port city in the northeast corner of the island. Patton found his task insulting. As the British plodded forward, he sent an American blitzkrieg to Palermo, in the north-central part of the island, barreling over German and Italian resistance, leaving enemy dead, destroyed panzers, and hoards of captured prisoners in his wake. His camera caught the action.

Patton took Palermo eleven days after coming ashore and was greeted by the Cardinal of Sicily. He soon settled into a 900-year-old castle where he enjoyed eating K-rations on fine china adorned with the cross of Saxony.

With the island effectively cut in half, Patton turned the Seventh Army towards Messina. When the British were bogged down on the east coast, he saw an excellent opportunity to beat them there. He pushed his Army east, often finding himself bombed or shelled along the way. He flanked the Germans three times with amphibious landings while the rest of his army pushed north, fighting the toughest battle of the campaign at Troina. Yet, despite the perils of combat and his unceasing drive to beat the British to Messina, Patton still found time to photograph his troops and the destruction they wrought. He reached Messina ahead of the British, proving the capabilities of the American soldier.

The Sicilian campaign marked a departure for Patton's photography. Whereas his North Africa pictures were of command posts and commanders, his Sicily photographs showed the war up close. There were numerous pictures of GIs and dead Germans. He noted that many pictures were taken while under fire. He also used photos as sketch pads, drawing arrows to denote specific points in a picture, a practice he began in North Africa. During the campaign he took no pictures of Sicily's Roman or Greek ruins. There would be time for that after the campaign.

With the Sicilian campaign concluded, Patton found himself out of a job. The U.S. Fifth Army, under Lt. Gen. Mark Clark, invaded Italy, using some of the Seventh Army's divisions. The rest of Patton's army was shipped off to the United Kingdom to prepare for the invasion of France. But that was not why he was left without a command. During the race for Messina, he had twice angrily slapped soldiers suffering from battle fatigue. These two incidents prompted a rebuke from Gen. Dwight D. Eisenhower, Patton's superior, who left him in a long and painful exile. From the heights of victory, Patton would find himself adrift in an uneasy limbo.

Patton adjusts his camera strap after wading ashore at Gela. His pants are still wet and he is under artillery and machine-gun fire. He considered the best picture of him during the Sicilian campaign.[1]

Patton directs the landings in an unposed photo (according to him). The African-American soldier to his right knew Patton when he was a lieutenant at Fort Riley, Kansas and went AWOL from his own unit to join the invasion.[2]

Landing craft head for the Gela beaches. Patton called these Higgins boats "the puppies."[3]

Navy shoremen try to push a landing craft off the beach at Gela.

This captured Italian flag was given to Patton by Lucian Truscott, the 3rd Infantry Division commander.

The campaign gets under way as American artillery opens up on the German lines.[4]

DISASTER IN THE SKIES ABOVE SICILY

On the night of July 11, a fleet of C-47s carrying the 504th Parachute Infantry Regiment of the 82nd Airborne Division approached Sicily to reinforce the troops already on the ground. Many never made it. Patton had done everything in his power to make sure the delivery of paratroops behind his own lines went off without a hitch. He contacted his commanders, both army and navy, and told them the time and direction of the air fleet's arrival, stressing he wanted the anti-aircraft units alerted to the friendly presence. Unfortunately, the Luftwaffe also decided to visit the American beachhead on Gela that day. Sortie after sortie bombed and strafed the beaches and naval craft all day. By the time the troop-laden American planes arrived over the beaches, men on the ground were edgy and frustrated.

Patton realized the possible danger of flying planes into an unstable area and tried to call off the flights around 8 PM but was unsuccessful. "Am terribly worried," he wrote in his diary.[1] His fears were justified. Moments after a German fighter flew out of the area, darting between two Allied ships as it left, the first wave of C-47s arrived. While the paratroopers jumped safely, the next wave was not as lucky. From the beaches, a lone machine gun within the perimeter of the green 45th Infantry Division opened up on the defenseless planes. Anti-aircraft gunners on the ground and the sea immediately followed suit.

A crescendo of fire tore into the planes. They scattered, dropping men behind enemy and Allied lines where they were fired on as the floated to the ground. Some planes returned to their airstrips with their full compliment of troopers. Twenty-three planes crashed into the island or splashed into the Mediterranean Sea. In all, 82 paratroopers were killed, 131 were wounded and 16 were missing.[2] When Gen. Dwight D. Eisenhower learned about the disaster he fired off a message to Patton demanding action for the "inexcusable carelessness and negligence on the part of someone." Eisenhower also reminded Patton who authorized

The spoils of war. This was the first big gun the Seventh Army captured in Gela. It was used in a counterattack on the second day of the campaign. Patton had a naval radio operator call in fire from the ships offshore to help stop the Axis attack.

Patton began taking pictures of dead Germans, writing on the photos "Good Hun" or "Good German" or, eventually, just "G.G." He never took pictures of dead Americans.[5]

the airdrop: "Before the beginning of this operation you particularly requested me to authorize this movement into your area." Ike could not understand what went wrong, since "ample time was obviously available for complete and exact coordination of the movement." He ordered Patton to launch an immediate investigation, and once the guilty person was found out, "I want a statement of the disciplinary action taken by you."[3]

Patton bristled at the note. He took it as a personal reprimand, saying Ike had cussed him out, and he resented it. Didn't Ike know he was fighting a battle here? Patton had warned all his corps and division commanders to get the word out to their soldiers, as well as all the ship captains in the water off Sicily. Despite all of his efforts, Patton was big enough to accept the blame, "but personally, I feel immune to censure," he confided to his diary. Unfortunately, Patton's demons began to haunt him at the same time: "Perhaps Ike is looking for an excuse to relieve me… If they want a goat, I am it."[4]

Patton's investigation turned up no traitors, no soldiers derelict of duty or anyone whose incompetence led to the tragedy. Instead, it was a number of factors: the commander of the 45th Infantry Division had failed to get the word out to everyone in the unit; the planes, trying to steer clear of the Luftwaffe, did not fly their prescribed course; some ground units failed to heed the orders not to fire on the planes; the airborne troops and the ground troops had different signs and countersigns; and recognition signals for the airborne troops and the ground troops were different.[5]

In the end, no one was punished and the event was covered up, lest it damage Allied morale. What it taught Patton, as well as Eisenhower, was that the fog of war is thick and the enemy does not always behave the way you might hope. The disaster over Sicily was an eventuality of the war, something that happens when armies clash. It would also not be the last friendly fire incident of World War II. ●

Agrigento. Patton captured the port town as a base for supplies in order to attack Palermo.

Another "good Hun." The Germans booby-trapped their dead, a practice Patton found disgusting and his soldiers found infuriating. The result, according to Patton, was fewer German prisoners taken and "more enemy dead than usual."[6]

(Left) "A very dead mule." The terrain in Sicily was so rough that mules were brought in to haul supplies.

Patton reviews the situation with Gen. Harold Alexander, the commander of the 15th Army Group.

(Above left) Ever the consummate tanker, Patton took a number of pictures of German tanks to check on the enemy's advances in technology. The arrows denote the extra armor on a Mark III tank.[7] (Above right) He was also interested in his own tanks. Here, Patton has placed five "Xs" where enemy shells hit an American Sherman tank.

Patton was unimpressed with the German Tiger tank. "In my opinion their so-called Tiger tanks with their 88mms are a flop. They are too slow."[8] Despite his low opinion, American M4 Sherman tanks could not knock out a Tiger in one-on-one combat. They were usually put out of action by artillery.[9]

An Army ambulance passes a knocked-out German tank. "The whole country is literally strewn with smashed trucks, guns, and tanks," Patton wrote.[10]

Palermo taken. Patton was relieved to find the harbor less damaged than originally reported, although most of the waterfront buildings were destroyed. Patton had resisted bombing to avoid killing civilians.[11]

Patton meets with Cardinal Lavitrano, the Cardinal of Sicily in Palermo.

To celebrate their general's victory, Patton's staff presented him with this Sicilian cart painted with images of his landing in Sicily and his meeting with the Cardinal.[12]

Patton's "little house," as he called it, in Palermo. He occupied the Royal Palace, which had been built in AD 1000 and contained oil paintings, a grand staircase, and gold furniture. Patton slept in the king's bedroom on three mattresses. The servants all gave him the fascist salute.[13]

Patton was proud of the Seventh Army's fighting spirit. "It was funny to see our men sitting down among the German corpses eating their lunch," he boasted.[14] Here a Seventh Army soldier takes a picture of Patton while Patton takes his. (Right) General Montgomery visits Patton at Palermo. Patton jokingly referred to him as "Monty of Palermo," and himself as "Monty's guard of honor."

Patton mugs for the camera on a veranda in Palermo.

The Germans blew up almost every bridge in their retreat to Messina to delay the Seventh Army. American engineers built this bridge using captured material.

This fort at Geraci was characteristic of Axis defenses. Patton called the terrain typical of the Sicilian countryside.

— PATTON'S OLD FRIEND, PADDY —

For Harry "Paddy" Flint, there was no age limit in war. Almost sidelined by his fifty-five years in 1943, he was visiting his friend George S. Patton's command post in Sicily when word came through that the commander of the 39th Infantry Regiment, 9th Infantry Division, had broken his leg. Flint soon showed up at the regimental headquarters telling people, "Georgie sent me."[1]

His advanced years were not apparent to his new troops. Already exhausted by their previous attempts to push the well-entrenched Germans from a hilltop position, the men were impressed as their new commander exposed himself to the enemy and taunted them. This little bow-legged colonel, wearing a black bandanna and wielding a rifle, seemed to fear nothing as he headed up the hill. The troops rose and followed him. It would not be the last time.

Flint was born in St. Johnsbury, Vermont, in 1886 and grew up fishing, trapping, and hunting. He attended Norwich University, where he ranked third in his class. He entered the Naval Academy in 1907 but resigned to attend West Point where he met Cadet George S. Patton. After graduation, he was assigned to the horse cavalry stationed at Fort Huachuca, Arizona, and later Hawaii. He was then stationed at Fort Riley, Kansas, but missed the Punitive Expedition into Mexico. He did make it to France for the Great War, however, serving with three different artillery units. When the guns went silent on November 11, 1918, Flint remained in Europe as part of the army of occupation for three more years.

In 1928, Flint served with Patton on a review board for an armored car. As war clouds gathered, Paddy was with Patton as Patton commanded the 2nd Armored Division, and he served as Patton's

Col. H.A. "Paddy" Flint, an old friend of Patton's, poses next to his headquarters. At Troina, Flint found his men stalled by the Germans, so he mounted a truck, rolled a cigarette with one hand and yelled, "Shoot, you bastards. You can't hit me!" He inspired his men to attack. Later they added "AAAO" to their helmets, signifying "Anytime, Anyplace, Anywhere, Bar Nothing." Patton took numerous pictures of Flint.[2]

aide during the Louisiana Maneuvers in 1941. But Paddy was over fifty years old and it looked like he would be left out of the war. Gen. George C. Marshall, the Chief of Staff of the Army, ended the Army's seniority system and began promoting younger officers. Patton reassured his friend that the army would change the age limit, and he was right. Paddy made it to North Africa with the 2nd Armored, putting in time as a staff officer at a number of posts.

His bravery made him an instant success with his men. When he saw the first reports of his actions at the front that said, "Some damn old fool is out front shooting his rifle like hell, exposing us

(CONTINUED)

────── **PADDY** (CONTINUED) ──────

all to retaliatory fire," Flint crossed out the word "old" and marked the paper for file. Shortly thereafter he aided a wounded soldier, then took the man's rifle and used it to take out a German machine gun.

Flint brought color and leadership to his position. When Patton asked him why he was with the infantry and not the cavalry, Flint replied "an infantryman ain't nothing but a cavalryman without his horse anyway." When he requested his men be allowed to wear the ~~AAAO~~ symbol on their helmets for "Anything, Anywhere, Anytime, Bar Nothing," which was strictly forbidden, his division commander asked Omar Bradley, the corps commander, if it was okay. Bradley, knowing of Flint's relationship with Patton, said, "I don't see a thing."[3]

With the completion of the Sicilian campaign, Flint took his regiment to the United Kingdom where he trained them along with the rest of the 9th Infantry Division. Patton was nearby but they were both too busy to visit. Flint promised to keep a "candle lit" at his headquarters, hoping his old friend would visit, and told Patton he looked forward to shaking his hand and hearing his belly laugh.

Flint made it to France before Patton, leading his men in the close fighting south of Cherbourg, where Flint led again from the front, often keeping his men ahead of schedule. When Bradley radioed Flint's division to see if they were ready for an Air Force attack prior to taking Quineville, word came back that "Paddy Flint and two companies have been in the center of town for two hours." Patton heard about Flint's exploits and wrote Bea, "Paddy's clearly nuts, but fights well."

That was Flint's style: he would find the front, advance out ahead of it and set up headquarters. He would bring in prisoners himself. Once, when he saw a small soldier trudging along carrying mortar equipment, he gave him a two-mile ride and told him to take a nap while the other men caught up with him. Patton wrote him saying, "I hope that you don't get killed, but if you do, there are many worse ways of dying and none of us can live forever." Ever the jokester, Patton told Flint that if he did die, he would make sure that he would be buried in a chestnut coffin so Flint could "go about cracking and snapping in hell."[4]

Ten days later Paddy was leading his men in house-to-house fighting when a German sniper shot him. He had just finished leading a tank he had come across with a disabled turret. "Don't tell me what you can't do!" the thin colonel railed at the tank driver. "It isn't often that you have a colonel for an escort, get started!"

Flint led the tank, carbine in hand and came back with bullet holes in his trousers. As he gave instructions to a sergeant on how to take up positions, a shot rang out and Flint fell forward; an enemy bullet had struck him in the right side of his helmet. The bullet did not penetrate but it dented the helmet, driving a thumb-sized piece of skull into Flint's brain. The men tended to the wound but there was little they could do. When someone spotted the sniper and took him out, Flint smiled. As his men prepared to move him to the rear, one of them told Flint, "You can't kill an Irishman, you can only make him mad." It was a final tribute to Flint. He died the next day.[5]

Patton never forgot his friend. At Flint's funeral Patton said, "I hope when it is my time to go, I go as gallantly and painlessly." A few days later he mailed Flint's helmet, map case and dispatch case to his widow, Sallie, and promised to send her pictures of the funeral ceremony. At the end of the war, in 1945, when Patton settled into his occupation headquarters in Bad Tölz, Germany, he renamed his headquarters Flint Kaserne in a final salute to his friend.[6] ●

During the race for Messina, Patton sent three amphibious attacks against the German rear, showing his ingenuity in offensive movement. This is one of the beach areas from which the attacks were conducted.

Patton confers with Maj. Gen. Lucian Truscott *(arrow)* as the Seventh Army heads east. Patton claimed, "This is where we actually planned the attack on Messina." During one roadside meeting with Truscott, three German planes bombed the road. Patton's only regret was that there were not enough spectators "to see how officers conduct themselves in tight positions."[15]

The fruits of victory. These German weapons are on their way to the U.S. Army's Aberdeen Proving Grounds in Maryland for engineers to study. Patton made special note of the muzzle break on the Mark IV tank on the left, the halftrack in the center with a 75 mm antitank gun in its well, and the 40 mm cannon on a Mark III chassis on the right, of which he commented, "I had no idea this particular weapon was effective."[16]

Patton congratulates the 1st Infantry Division for a job well done in Sicily.

Mission accomplished. Some of the Seventh Army's troops leave Sicily for England. "The future of the Seventh Army does not look bright," Patton confessed. Soon things would dim also for Patton, as he found himself in exile for his actions during the race to Messina.[17]

IV
LIMBO

During the race to Messina, Patton visited two field hospitals. In each he found a soldier suffering from battle fatigue, which he considered simple cowardice. He lost control and delivered a tongue-lashing, then slapped the men. The two incidents tainted the Sicily victory and haunted Patton for the next six months. The incidents resulted in a reprimand from Eisenhower, followed by Patton's public apologies to the Seventh Army, unit by unit.

With nothing to do, and to console himself, Patton toured Sicily, visiting sites of battles old and new, making a photographic record of even the most minute details of architecture and terrain. Often, he found his sites by flying over them in a Piper Cub he sometimes piloted himself. He was impressed with the ancient ruins that dotted the hilltops, writing that he could "almost see the Greeks walking up and down the hill." When not touring, he kept tabs on the slow progress of Gen. Mark Clark's Italian campaign, hoping to be called back into action at any moment.

He sent Beatrice a number of "blood and guts" pictures, and some color pictures. He also received two new cameras, one from Beatrice and one from Mrs. Polly Case, who was visiting Sicily. Her husband was the head of the Eastman Kodak Company.[1]

Although sitting on the sidelines, Patton was still important to Allied strategy. Eisenhower sent him around the Mediterranean to keep the Germans guessing as to where the Allies would attack next. The Germans considered Patton the Allies' best battlefield commander and, they thought that wherever Patton was, the next assault was sure to come.

Patton visited Corsica, Cairo, Jerusalem, and Malta, snapping pictures at each spot. In Corsica he visited Napoleon Bonaparte's birthplace, inspected troops, airfields, and harbors, and, of course, took pictures. He referred to his trip to North Africa as his "Cairo farce," and reviewed the impressive Polish corps while there. He drove to the spot where Jesus Christ was believed to have risen to heaven and noted that "four Secret Service men protected me while visiting all the Holy places—lack of faith?" He also visited the pyramids but was unimpressed, considering them smaller than the ones he had seen in Mexico.[2]

In early January 1944, Patton went to Italy to visit his friends fighting with the Fifth Army. While touring the front lines, he was walking down a hill when he stopped to take a picture of artillery guns firing in a field. As he snapped away, four German shells crashed into the road where he would have been had he not stopped to take the pictures. Another two shells struck the top of the hill where he had been. Metal fragments flew past Patton and his staff, but no one was injured. He considered the enemy volley "nice, as they all arrived together and were well grouped." Once again, Patton's luck held, reassuring his belief in his own destiny to fight again.[3]

Returning to Sicily, Patton visited two ancient temples. The first, the temple of Himera, dated back to around 395 BC. He had been searching for it since first arriving in

After the Sicilian campaign, Patton took to the air to take pictures of his army's achievements. This Bailey bridge was constructed after the Germans destroyed the original during the race for Messina. Patton referred to the sharply rising hills as "typical of island terrain."[4]

Sicily. The next day he visited the temple of Apollo, which he felt "must have been very magnificent but was never finished." He took many photographs at each site.[5]

Finally, in the last week of January, Patton received the call to return to the war. Slated to command the Third Army, he flew to England to accept his new assignment. Soon he was off to Knutsford to take the command. He moved into Peover Hall, where he prepared for the invasion of France.

He visited his troops, delivering rousing speeches full of battlefield lessons and motivation, ending each by reminding the men that he was not there, for his presence in England was still secret. To familiarize the men with Allied aircraft, he ordered whole divisions to watch individual planes circle and dive from above. He even accompanied a British Mosquito on one such flyover, photographing the men on the ground.[6]

With the war over in Sicily but continuing in Italy, a number of Patton's men were called to command there. Gen. Geoffrey Keyes, Patton's deputy commander and the man who had led the race to Palermo, left Patton in early October to take over II Corps in Italy. Patton titled this picture, "Off to Battle."[7]

For company, Patton purchased a bull terrier he named Willie. The dog was constantly at his master's side: in his headquarters, while visiting troops or, later, on the battlefield. Patton adored Willie and sent home numerous photos of the dog.

But just as things began looking up, Patton got into trouble again. His presence in England was still a secret when he addressed a group of British volunteers—mostly women—who had organized a welcoming club for American soldiers. Pictures of him there and his remarks were made public by the British press, blowing his cover. Then the press misquoted him, claiming that he had not included the Soviet Union in a statement regarding Great Britain and the United States as post-war rulers. While the press in the United States played up the speech blunder, Eisenhower worried that Patton's propensity for self-promotion could ruin his need to remain unknown.

D-Day occurred without Patton. He chafed at being left out of the invasion of Europe, jealous that all the attention going to Bradley and Eisenhower. "Omar takes Ernie

Pyle and a camera man with him always but does nothing to record," he wrote to Beatrice. "Destiny [Eisenhower] has two still and two movie men with him."[8]

Finally, on July 6, his wait was over. With German V-bombs falling on London and making Patton uncomfortable, he boarded a plane bound for Normandy, France. He would soon be back in action.

To disguise the location of the next Allied landings from the Germans, Eisenhower sent Patton around the Mediterranean. In Corsica he visited the birthplace of his hero, Napoleon Bonaparte, where he touched the couch where the French emperor was born. Here, he stands outside the birthplace, which he referred to as "seats of the mighty," with French Gen. Alphonse Juin (center).[9]

For his second birthday of the war Patton visited a cemetery for the 2nd Armored Division. He lamented that the year before he had captured Casablanca. "Now I command little more than my self-respect."

Patton's "Cairo Farce" begins. He snapped this picture of his staff: Gen. Hobart Gay is in the center, Col. Charles Codman is fourth from the left.[10]

Patton next went to the Holy Land where he shot this picture of the mosque built on the spot where Jesus Christ ascended to heaven. Ever the comedian, Patton added, "Hell of a note."[11]

Patton places a Seventh Army patch on the shoulder of Polish Gen. Wladyslaw Anders, the commander of the II Polish Corps, then stationed in Egypt. Anders told Patton that if his corps were attacked by both the Russians and Germans, "they would have difficulty in deciding which they wanted to fight the most."

Patton and the pyramids: Although he was initially thrilled to see the pyramids when his plane flew over them, he was less than impressed when he got up close, commenting in his diary that they seemed smaller than the ones he had seen in Mexico City. The most significant aspect of the area to him was only that his hero, "Napoleon had been there."[12]

Snake charmer coaxes his pet in Karnak, Egypt.

Patton's entourage checks out the tomb of Ramses II, whom Patton considered "a new deal Pharaoh of 1400 BC."[13]

In Malta, Patton visited castles and forts that date back to the sixteenth century. He noted that the knights who occupied them had taken a vow of poverty, chastity and obedience. "They only kept the last vow."[14]

— A SLAPPED SOLDIER'S STORY —

Patton almost lost his position in the Army—and history—because of slapping two soldiers during one of his most stunning victories. Palermo had been captured and Patton's Seventh Army was now closing in on Messina, the last German stronghold on the northeastern-most tip of Sicily. Patton wanted to prove that American soldiers were the equal of, if not better than, their British counterparts, and only beating them to Messina could do that.

On August 2, 1943, Patton was visiting a field hospital when he encountered Pvt. Charles H. Kuhl. "Patton came in and all the soldiers jumped to attention except me," recalled Kuhl in a 1970 interview with the *Indiana Tribune.* "I was suffering from battle fatigue and didn't know what to do."

Patton, accompanied by members of his staff and some doctors, worked his way down the rows of beds, talking to the men and especially commending the wounded. When he got to Kuhl, Patton asked him why he hadn't gotten up and saluted. "I told him my nerves were shot and of course I didn't feel like getting up to salute him."

Patton became enraged and immediately began berating Kuhl. Somewhere in the profanities Patton was blasting at him, Kuhl thought he heard Patton say: "I don't know how a mother could raise such a sissy or coward!" Yelling at him to get back to his unit, Patton smacked Kuhl across his face with a pair of gloves he was holding. He then grabbed Kuhl by the scruff of his neck and headed him for the door. "As I started out the door of the receiving tent, he kicked me in the fanny."

Kuhl hid out in a ward tent until Patton left. He was readmitted and found to have malaria. Kuhl, a soldier in the 1st Infantry Division, had seen action in North Africa before fighting in Sicily. He later participated in the Normandy invasion but was relieved after ten days of combat after suffering another bout of battle fatigue. "I think the guy [Patton] was also suffering from battle fatigue," Kuhl reflected twenty-seven years after the incident. "He seemed about halfway nuts to me at the time."

Kuhl tried to put the incident behind him and forget about it. He returned home to Indiana after the war and got a job as a scrubber with the Bendix Corporation, a manufacturing facility. But when the movie *Patton* came out he had to relive the experience anew. "The whole experience is still nerve-wracking," he told his interviewer in 1970. The strain may have been too much for him—he died ten months later. ●

Patton and General Keyes inspect the front lines of Keyes's II Corps in Italy in January.

During his visit to the Italian front, Patton walked down a hill to take this picture of artillery guns firing on a war-torn field. As he snapped the picture, an artillery barrage crashed into the road thirty feet ahead. The picture, he wrote, "saved my life."[15]

The rounds that missed. This is where Patton would have been standing had he not taken the previous photo. Two other shells landed on the road. A fragment from the explosion hit Col. Charles Codman in the helmet, and the nose of a shell landed nine inches from Patton's foot. He felt the lord had spared him for future glory. The incident, he wrote, "gives me great confidence."[16]

Before leaving Sicily, Patton toured the temple of Himera, or what was left of it after the Carthaginians destroyed it in 405 BC. He had been searching for the temple since first landing in Sicily seven months earlier.[17]

Gen. Hobart Gay stands amid the ruins of the temple of Apollo, the largest temple in Sicily. Patton considered the columns "perfectly stupendous," and calculated that their separate sections weighed at least ten tons each.[18]

Back in command. Upon arrival in England, Patton took command of the Third Army. He set up his headquarters in Peover Hall near the town of Knutsford. He described his residence as "a huge house last repaired in 1627 or thereabouts."[19]

(Left) To train his troops in identifying aircraft, Patton arranged to have Allied planes fly over troop formations. In this instance, he went airborne in a British Mosquito bomber that circled above the men at 300 mph before diving once. The experience gave Patton an appreciation of a fighter pilot's job: "It is very difficult to recognize ground forms."[20] (Right) Maj. Gen. John "P" Wood, commander of the 4th Armored Division. Patton would owe much to Wood and his brilliant attacks during the breakout in France.

PATTON UNDER FIRE

Patton constantly exposed himself to enemy fire. During the North Africa landings he was on the deck of the USS *Augusta* while it dueled with the Vichy French Navy, and he was strafed by French fighter planes on the beach. As the commander of the II Corps in Tunisia he was constantly under German artillery fire. In Sicily he was strafed and shot at again and even stood his ground during an Axis counterattack at Gela. On his visit to Italy in January 1944, a German artillery barrage just missed him, and in England he could hear explosions from impacting V1 and V2 rockets. Throughout Europe he was usually within range of German small arms fire and was once almost killed by an Allied fighter plane that mistook his plane for a German aircraft.

But there is one incident he never wrote about or spoke of. A month before D-Day, Patton was sitting in the copilot seat of his C-47 transport plane flying over the Irish Sea headed for Prestwick, Scotland. In the plane with him were the pilot, Eldin Onsgard, the co-pilot, who was sitting in the back, and Patton's dog, Willie. The C-47 had no fighter escort since it was flying over Allied territory far from enemy shores. Suddenly, a German Focke-Wulf 190 fighter pounced, coming in at a steep angle nose to nose with the C-47. Onsgard took evasive action, dropping the landing gear, putting on full flaps and pulling back on both engines. The German, not prepared for such a quick slow-down, shot in front of the C-47 and screamed past.

Onsgard knew his tricky maneuvering would not save the plane a second time—they were sitting ducks. But Patton's luck held again. As the 190 pulled out of its dive, it came under fire from a ship below. Anti-aircraft fire tore into it, bringing it down. The sudden rush of excitement unnerved Onsgard, who began shaking. Patton just turned to him and said, "Make a report on that."[1]

Why did Patton ignore the incident? Possibly because he was just coming out of the shadow of the Knutsford incident and felt that he had just saved his career. To be brought down helplessly in a transport plane without firing a shot was not the way he wanted to go, not with a major campaign only a month away. Months later, when he came under fire from an Allied fighter, he joked about it, having already proven himself on the battlefields of Europe. ●

ENTER WILLIE

In March, Patton bought himself a white fifteen-month-old bull terrier, Punch, whose owner, a Royal Air Force pilot, had been killed over Europe. Patton renamed the dog Willie. The pet would become the focus of many a Patton picture.[21]

Willie accompanies Patton on an inspection of the Third Army. "Willie is crazy about me," Patton would boast. "He snores too." The terrier even had combat experience: his previous owner had taken him on a raid over Berlin.[22]

Willie kills a small rabbit at Peover Hall. Patton described his terrier as white except for a dark lemon-colored spot on his tail, "which at cursory glance would seem to indicate that he had not used toilet paper."[23]

Willie waits for his master on the training fields of England.

Patton shows off Willie before leaving on an engagement with his staff.

Willie leaps over a wall "like an Irish terrier," according to Patton.[24]

Willie at rest.

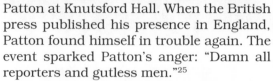

Patton at Knutsford Hall. When the British press published his presence in England, Patton found himself in trouble again. The event sparked Patton's anger: "Damn all reporters and gutless men."[25]

(Right) Ready for war: Patton prepares to fly from England to France exactly one month after the D-Day landings. He noted that it was the same date he left North Africa for the invasion of Sicily a year before. With German V-1 "buzz bombs" raining down on London—six landing within earshot the day before he left—he admitted, "I shall be glad to be out of here and one stage nearer the war."[26]

V
FRANCE

When Patton landed at Omaha Beach in Normandy, he became the focus of other photographers. The troops there began taking his picture. "Mostly soldiers with $5.00 Leicas," he noticed. "But there were some professionals present whom I warned off by assuring them I was still a secret."[1]

The Germans continued to box in the Allied armies in the Normandy area as men and supplies built up on the invasion beaches. With little to do until the Third Army became operational, Patton took pictures of his mobile headquarters and a V-1 missile-launching site. He went aloft several times in his Piper Cub to study the terrain and take more pictures, once flying over the German lines. He also helped in the ad hoc development of metal cutters, so tanks could slice through the hedgerows, walls of earth, rocks, and trees that divided French farms into a checkerboard countryside.[2]

To break free of the hedgerows, Gen. Omar Bradley devised Operation Cobra, a massive air bombardment followed by a ground attack. On July 25, 1944, more than 2,400 bombers and fighter-bombers struck the German lines, destroying defenses, smashing tanks and killing scores of the enemy. Some bombs, however, fell short, killing and wounding hundreds of Americans. The dead included Lt. Gen. Leslie McNair, Patton's friend. But the breach was made. Infantry and armor poured through the gap, setting the stage for Patton's exploits. After the bombardment, Patton and Bradley went up in their Piper Cubs. Patton pointed his lens at the destruction and took a picture of the spot where McNair was killed.[3]

With the German lines pulverized and the enemy confused, Patton put his tanks to work. His armored divisions smashed through the front lines and rolled through the countryside, splitting into three directions. Patton's amazing advance surprised friend and foe alike, and he cheered every time he ran off one map and had to use another.[4]

As his army rolled through France with dizzying speed and pivoted north toward Paris, Patton indulged in some historical sightseeing. He stopped by Château de Fougeres, which had been destroyed in the early 1600s when Cardinal Richelieu crushed the Huguenots. Patton took pictures of the castle and posed for a few more. But the breakout gave him little time for extensive picture-taking. Most of the photos he took were of fellow commanders visiting his field headquarters.

Although blocked from entering Paris by a change in army boundaries, Patton's lightning advance made taking the city possible. Heading east, he resorted to flying to his corps and division command posts, often taking pictures of his army's progress.

As more and more French soil was liberated, Patton came into familiar territory. He visited sites he remembered from World War I, where he either had stayed or fought. He sent photographs to Army Chief of Staff Gen. George Marshall, who had served with the American forces in 1918. Patton sought out Marshall's former landlady and his old headquarters, snapping away and explaining to Marshall that he personally took the pictures: "This probably accounts for their being as bad as they are."[5] He also sent pictures to his old commander from World War I, Gen. John J. Pershing. The pictures, along with kind letters, may have been an attempt to reestablish contact with his old commander and mentor, who had stopped writing to him after the slapping incidents in Sicily.

At the end of August, Patton's progress slowed. In his race across France, he had outrun his fuel supplies. In fact, the entire Allied army faced a logistical crisis, with poor weather and stiffening German resistance adding to the slowdown. Even an airborne and tank assault led by British field marshal Montgomery could not breach the front. Yet Patton kept pushing forward and killing Germans. On September 13, he crossed the Moselle River. After taking a picture of the event, he climbed into a foxhole and watched a tank battle only yards away. He took pictures of the men in the trench.[6]

October saw much of the same kind of fighting as Patton laid siege to the fortress city of Metz. Generals Eisenhower and Marshall visited on two different occasions, and

Patton collected the Signal Corps pictures of their visits and sent them to Beatrice.[7] Throughout the campaign, he kept up the pressure on the Germans. On October 8, he visited the front near the town of Nancy. While fighters and bombers attacked the German lines, he "secured," as he put it, pictures of the front with a telephoto lens, checking off German locations on one of the prints.[8]

As Patton pushed forward, the Germans introduced a new weapon to the front: a 280 mm rail gun. Shells began falling at night. "They have not had much luck," he commented. On the night of October 24, their luck improved. Two shells landed on a dwelling thirty feet from Patton's house, shattering his windows. Awakened by Willie, Patton ran across the street and helped dig an old man and a little girl from the rubble. "Do not worry," an old woman shouted to the

Patton conducted his breakout and pursuit strategy from this mobile headquarters, which had room for a bed, desk, radio, wash stand, and map room. He worried that the truck was too comfortable and would make him soft.[10]

trapped girl. "The great General Patton is helping to dig you out!" Once he made sure everyone was safe, he took a picture of the caved-in roof.[9]

As his army tried to resume the offensive, Patton was at the front. In early November he watched as a thousand bombers flew over Metz and dropped their deadly cargoes on the German lines. "I took some pictures which may be of some interest," he told Beatrice.[11] He spent the rest of the month visiting his divisions, where he took pictures of men crossing the Saar and laying siege to Metz.

The photos of France, much like the pictures taken in North Africa and Sicily, combined the present war with the past. And, of course, there were the images of his commanders. New to the pictures was humor: cartoons from soldiers and some humorous quotes added to his picture with Marshall. The next two months would see Patton's greatest challenges and greatest successes, but little time for picture-taking.

The headquarters even included a simple—and immodest— 25-gallon outdoor shower. Inside, the mobile head-quarters was gas-heated, which gave Patton headaches, forcing him to turn it off and sleep in the cold.[12]

While waiting to take command of the Third Army, Patton visited a German V1 rocket launch site in Normandy. Even though most of the structure was underground, he thought the device "stupendous" and compared it to a pyramid. He did admit, though, "I could not figure out how it worked," and that pictures could not do justice to the structure's size.[13]

Captured German Generalleutnant Karl Spang is escorted to Patton's head-quarters for questioning. He was amazed at the dignity and courtesy with which Patton's men treated him.[14]

(Left) To break through the dreaded hedgerows of Normandy, Patton aided in the development of these metal cutters attached to the fronts of tanks. The device enabled tanks to smash through hedgerows without exposing their thin armor bottoms. (Right) The result of a hedgerow-cutting tank. Patton planned to use the new device in a tank-led attack, followed by armored infantry and covered by time fire. "My plan is very simple and direct, and I think that all those present approved of it."[15]

ABOVE THE HEDGEROWS

After the Operation Cobra air bombardment, Patton and Bradley took to the sky in Piper Cubs. Flying made Patton feel like a "clay pigeon." To take his mind off his anxieties, he photographed Bradley's plane as well as knocked-out German tanks and dead cows, which he complained "smell[ed] to high heaven, or at least 300 feet high, as that was my altitude."

(Right) A number of dead cows lay in the fields of Normandy.

(Below) General Bradley's plane.

Patton took a picture of the bombed-out area where his friend, Lt. Leslie McNair, was killed when American bombs fell short on the American lines. Patton marked an "X" where McNair was killed.

(Left) Results of the bomber blitz. Patton was unimpresed with the extent of hte bombing, considering it sparse compared with the battlefields of World War I, "where it was physically possible to step from one shell hole to the next."[16]

(Right) Patton called this a dead Panther (German tank), but it looks more like a Sherman tank blown onto its side.

The speed with which Patton charged across France allowed for some levity in higher headquarters. On August 8, the Plans Section of General Bradley's Twelfth Army Group sent Patton this cartoon, showing their struggles at keeping up with his progress.[17]

As the Third Army began the breakout from the Cotentin peninsula, Patton visited Château de Fougères. He considered it the best fortress he had ever seen because it had not been lived in or improved upon since being destroyed in the early 1600s. "It had only been taken twice until we took it."[18]

Patton planned the liberation of Paris at his headquarters at the Château de Bois Gaunats in Laval. The "X" denotes the drawing room where the attack was organized. Madame Bouvilles, the owner of the château, later wrote Beatrice that the German Luftwaffe had previously occupied her home, but that the fourteen American generals, 600 officers and 1,300 soldiers of the Third Army at the chateau showed "such perfect discipline!"[19]

As Patton raced beyond Paris, he took to flying to his various commands. He stopped in Orléans, where he could see enemy artillery fire. He was proud to report that the local airport "broke a world's record by receiving and dispatching 600 planes yesterday, with 1,500 tons of supplies." Bomb craters can be seen in the lower right.[20]

Patton then moved on to Bourg, where he visited "my old house, my billet, and the chateau of Madame de Vaux, an acquaintance from World War I, and took pictures." He sent many of the pictures to Pershing, his World War I commander, who had not written Patton since the slapping incidents.[21]

When General Marshall asked Patton to have someone check on his landlady from World War I, Patton went personally, only to discover that she had moved to the south of France. He also visited Marshall's old headquarters in Chaumont and posed outside of it.[22]

Meeting MacArthur in World War I

After the liberation of Paris, Patton visited his old haunts from the First World War whenever the opportunity arose. He stopped by his old living quarters, Gen. Jack Pershing's headquarters, George C. Marshall's place, and the train yard where he had personally driven French tanks (American war industry had not produced any war-ready tanks in 1918) off the train cars for his men to train.

One place he did not visit, however, was where he met had Douglas MacArthur—at the time only a brigadier general—during the battle of St. Mihiel. After both men's deaths, some controversy would arise about what exactly took place during their meeting.

It was September 12, 1918, and the Americans were closing the St. Mihiel bulge in their lines. Patton, then a thirty-two-year-old lieutenant colonel in charge of the 327th Tank Battalion, and Douglas MacArthur, a thirty-eight-year-old brigadier general commanding the 84th Infantry Brigade, greeted each other on a small, exposed hill. On either side of them infantry and tanks maneuvered forward to the town of Essey. Small-arms fire and occasional artillery kept the air alive and dangerous. As Patton and MacArthur spoke, a German artillery barrage exploded up ahead and shells began marching towards their position. Infantrymen scattered and dove for cover, but the two officers remained standing, coolly talking to each other.

What happened next has been the subject of controversy ever since. According to Patton, who wrote about the encounter four days later, "I met General MacArthur commanding a brigade; he was walking about, too. I joined him and the creeping barrage came along towards us, but it was very thin and not dangerous. I think each one wanted to leave but each hated to do so, so we let it come over us.

We stood and talked but neither was much interested in what the other said as we could not get our minds off the shells." He wrote this account to his wife which, despite all its bombast, managed to be magnanimous to MacArthur's unwillingness to seek shelter. "I was the only man on the front line except for General MacArthur who never ducked a shell."[1]

MacArthur's version of the story is more convoluted. In his memoirs, *Reminiscences,* completed forty-seven years after the fact, MacArthur dedicates only two sentences to the incident: "We were followed by a squadron of tanks, which soon bogged down in the heavy mud. The squadron was commanded by an old friend, who in another war was to gain world-wide fame, Maj. George S. Patton."[2] MacArthur's memoirs are a bit self-serving and tend to mention everyone's failings but his own. Thus it is no surprise that the only thing he mentions about Patton are his tank problems. He also errs by calling Patton a major, not a lieutenant colonel.

The different versions do not end there. In 1961, Jack Pearl, a writer of articles, commercials and early television scripts, wrote a book, *Blood-and-Guts Patton,* for the Monarch American Series. According to Pearl, Patton walked up to MacArthur and saluted, but caught himself ducking from a nearby shell. MacArthur then told Patton, "Don't sweat over 'em, Colonel. If they're gonna get you, they're gonna get you." When Patton asked him about the situation up ahead, MacArthur offered: "Why don't you go up ahead and have a look around?" Patton then climbed onto a tank to ride into Essey.[3]

Pearl's account contains two disputable points. First, there is little proof that Patton would catch

(CONTINUED)

Patton visits the headquarters of the American Expeditionary Force during World War I in Chaumont.

MEETING MACARTHUR (CONTINUED)

himself ducking during the encounter since Patton, by his own account, earlier in the day admitted to the uselessness of such an action: "I admit that I wanted to duck and probably did at first, but soon saw the futility of dodging fate."[4] Second, Patton did not ride a tank into Essey. Again, by his own account, he walked into Essey, but he did ride a tank into the next town. "When we got to Pannes some two miles [away] the infantry would not go in so I told the Sgt. commanding the tank to go in. He was nervous at being alone so I said I would sit on the roof. I got on top of the tank to hearten the driver. This reassured him and we entered the town."[5] Even though Pearl seems to quote directly from the two officers, his management of the facts and places seriously calls into question his reliability as a reporter.

Jack Pearl's version of the event was challenged later that year—by Pearl himself! After completing the book on Patton, Pearl wrote *General Douglas MacArthur,* again for the Monarch American Series. This time, rather than MacArthur's com-

ment, "Don't sweat over 'em, Colonel. If they're gonna get you, they're gonna get you," Pearl credits MacArthur with saying: "Don't worry, Colonel, you never hear the one that gets you." He also elaborates on the conversation. When MacArthur sees how disheartened Patton is from the "ribbing" the infantry brass is giving him as his tanks wallow in the mud, MacArthur offers: "Don't let them get you down, Colonel. These tanks of yours will dominate the character of war for the next hundred years." Patton responds, "I'm grateful someone besides me thinks so, sir." Not only does MacArthur appear paternal to Patton in this version, he also shows himself to be a great military visionary.[6] In neither version does Pearl cite his sources for the quotes, again creating serious doubt of their validity.

Pearl's "MacArthur" version of the story was next picked up by Jules Archer in 1963. In Archer's *Front-Line General: Douglas MacArthur,* Pearl's story of the Patton-MacArthur meeting was used but again, the quotes were not cited. Only the bib-

(Left) Charles Codman poses before the airfield he used to fly from during World War I. (Right) When the Third Army crossed the Moselle River in mid-September, Patton drove over the pontoon bridge then got out and photographed his command jeep.[23]

liography traces the quote to Pearl.[7] For some reason, Archer's version of the story seemed to legitimize it, as historian William Manchester later repeated the quotes in *American Caesar: Douglas MacArthur, 1880–1964,* citing Archer as the source. Geoffrey Perret's *Old Soldiers Never Die* and Stanley Hirshson's *General Patton: A General's Life* also fall into the Archer trap. Only D. Clayton James, in his three-volume biography on MacArthur, refused to use the exciting but fictitious quotes.

One Patton biographer does hold up a warning flag, questioning the dramatic versions of both Pearl and Archer. Carlo D'Este, author of *Patton: A Genius for War,* was probably unaware of Archer's version when he described Manchester's account as "nonsense." He may have thought that Manchester actually interviewed MacArthur for his book because D'Este blames the false story on MacArthur's faulty memory, "with the result that he and his biographer incorrectly identify Patton as a major."[8]

Whatever was actually said between the two was probably remembered by neither. The rain of artillery and other sounds of the battlefield made a deafening noise. While both men regarded their own personal histories in high esteem, they probably never thought the few words they exchanged on that hill would ever be considered important. Besides, they were both more concerned about moving men and machines forward than with their chat.

Patton's version of the story is probably more accurate since it was written so soon after the event. MacArthur's is more aloof and clouded in mystery. He is even patronizing, mentioning that the tanks were following his infantry. As for author Jack Pearl, he is said to have served as a military policeman in North Africa, Sicily, and Italy, but there is no evidence he ever spoke to Patton, much less MacArthur. The fact that Pearl changes MacArthur's quotes from one book to the next, within the same year, dissolves his credibility. ●

After crossing the river Patton visited this division observation post, where he watched a "lovely" tank battle about 1,500 yards away. He saw two German tanks burning while four American tanks, with guns blazing, attacked into the woods. Patton noticed that he could hear the difference between the American and German machine guns' rates of fire. "It was all very merry." [24]

Patton visited a regimental command post where Lt. Col. Christian Clark presented him with a captured German dagger with "Alles für Deutschland" engraved on it. Patton knew Clark before the war, in Hawaii, where Clark had served as an assistant to Gen. Hugh Drum, one of Patton's polo partners.[25]

Not all of Patton's pictures were of a serious nature. When Army Chief of Staff Gen. George C. Marshall visited Patton's headquarters near Metz, the two posed for this photograph, which Patton later improved upon.

The next day Patton visited the front to witness the attack on Nancy. He took this close-up picture of the action using a telephoto lens. This was a direct hit on a tire factory. Pilots who flew over the area later told Patton that the column of smoke was 4,000 feet high.[26]

Later in the attack, Patton noticed that the Germans still possessed one hill. He ordered a tank attack to capture it. Here, he marked the German outposts with check marks.

While driving between his and Bradley's headquarters, Patton visited the train station at Clermont where, in 1918, he detrained his tanks for the Meuse-Argonne offensive of World War I. Major Stiller, who served with him at the time, is to his left.[27]

During the fighting in October, Patton had his picture taken while he was photographing a flamethrower tank. "I look like Nita," he wrote Beatrice. (Nita was Patton's sister.) The camera is in Patton's left hand.

While visiting one of his Corps headquarters, Patton saw this dud fired from a 280 mm railgun. The spent shell is four and a half feet long.[28]

"I nearly lost the Third Army this morning by getting killed," he wrote to Beatrice. The Germans shelled his quarters in Nancy with the same railgun, three rounds crashing near his house, shattering all his windows and demolishing this dwelling thirty feet away. Patton ran outside and personally helped pull an old man and a little girl out of this wreckage. "I was really scared," he admitted.[29]

─────────── DECISION IN LORRAINE ───────────

On November 8, Patton visited Maj. Gen. Manton Eddy to witness the jump-off at Metz. While there, an army photographer took pictures of Patton and Eddy. Brig. Gen. Eric Wood, who was present, commented on these photos: "A decision by him [Patton] was necessary. He stood as shown (beside Eddy) without moving, looking into space for perhaps three minutes. Then he turned to General Eddy and gave his decision, leaving the O.P. [Observation Post] immediately thereafter."[30]

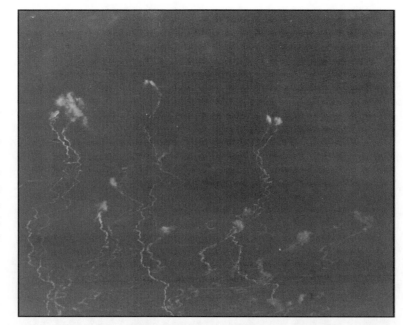

During the battle, Patton watched as a thousand bombers attacked the fortified areas of Metz. The bombardment was so heavy that he felt the ground shake. The picture shows target markers falling over the German lines.[31]

— PATTON'S CAMERA GOES HOLLYWOOD —

The most popular image of Patton is actually that of actor George C. Scott standing before an oversized American flag reciting Patton quotes on war and fighting. In the movie *Patton,* Scott almost perfectly replicated the General, right down to the bad teeth, the mole near his left eye, and the ruby ring he wore on the pinky of his left hand.[40]

Missing from most scenes, however, was the General's camera. The camera is prominent in only two scenes in the movie. When Patton arrives at II Corps headquarters in North Africa and meets with Omar Bradley (played by Karl Malden), he begins to take off his dusty coat and equipment while the two discuss the American defeat at Kasserine Pass. The camera, in its leather case, is one of the first things Patton takes off.

The camera is more prominent during the Battle of the Bulge sequence of the film. As the movie climaxes with the Third Army pushing toward Bastogne, Patton stands on a small rise with Colonel Codman and another, unidentified colonel to Patton's left. Snow falls as men, tanks and vehicles maneuver past. The camera dangles from Patton's neck as he extols the exploits of the Third Army, concluding his monologue with, "God! God, I'm proud of these men!"

It is strange that the camera appears during the Battle of the Bulge, the time that Patton took the fewest pictures in the course of the war, yet the camera is nowhere to be seen where he took the most pictures—Sicily and France. Often, Patton wore his camera across his chest, but even that could have been a distraction from the movie's martial theme. The producers may have felt it detracted from Patton's warrior image and made him look more like a tourist. Scott looked more impressive with a pair of binoculars dangling from his neck than he would have looked snapping pictures of his troops fighting their way into Palermo or Bastogne. ●

Patton spent his birthday, November 11, 1944, "getting where the dead were still warm." He enjoyed his day by snapping this photograph of a recently captured German self-propelled gun. Patton's shadow is in the foreground.[32]

Patton was not only interested in how his army fought, but how all its elements worked in a battle. Here a tank retriever pulls a "wounded" Sherman to the rear.

Metz taken! American tanks can be seen in the ditch and in the foreground. "I think that only Attila and the Third Army have ever taken Metz by assault."[33]

Patton refused to take certain pictures. When his troops captured Metz on November 22, they caught SS Brigadefuehrer Anton Dunckern, the highest-ranking SS officer captured thus far. Patton personally interrogated him. "I always wear high boots," he grinned, "when I talk to SS bastards." After the interview, in which Patton repeatedly berated the prisoner, a Signal Corps photographer took this picture, which Patton sent to Beatrice.[34]

VI
THE BATTLE OF THE BULGE

The Battle of the Bulge began for Patton almost three weeks before the Germans exploded out of the Ardennes Forest. On November 25, he confided in his diary that the First Army was making a mistake by not keeping the VIII Corps active, as he suspected that German forces were moving to the east.[1] That same day he took pictures of troops fighting. As he continued pushing his Army forward, and taking pictures of its progress, the possibility of a German counter-offensive continued to haunt him.

On December 16, nineteen German divisions smashed into the American line in the Ardennes Forest, forcing the Americans back. The next day General Bradley telephoned Patton and ordered him to give up one of his armored divisions for the crisis in the Ardennes. Patton protested, as he was about to launch his own attack into Germany. But he relented. [2]

As the Germans pushed forward, they surrounded Bastogne, where the 101st Airborne Division and elements of other units blocked the town. The invested city had to be relieved and Patton was up to the task. Within days, despite heavy snow and a lack of air cover because of fog, he turned his Army north and attacked towards Bastogne. To bolster his men's spirits, and to break the nasty weather that impeded his army, he issued a prayer, to be presented to all the men of the Third Army on Christmas Day. The next day the weather cleared and the first tanks of the Third Army made contact with Bastogne's defenders. Patton considered the Bastogne operation his "biggest and best."[3]

Patton was too busy pushing his army forward and grappling with the enemy for picture-taking. Instead, he supplemented the pictures he sent home with an array of Signal Corps photographs, some with crop marks on them from the *Stars and Stripes* newspaper. He picked pictures that showed GIs in their environment: eating rations, repairing machines, and posing by knocked-out enemy tanks.[4] He also collected a number of gun camera pictures from fighter aircraft that blasted the Germans on open roads. To give Beatrice a more accurate picture of what was happening, he also sent home a number of colored maps showing the various stages of the liberation of Bastogne. Each showed friendly forces in blue and enemy forces in red.

But the relief of Bastogne did not signal the end of the Battle of the Bulge. Patton still had to help close the Bulge and then turn east to keep pressure on the retreating Germans. Again, he was constantly on the move in an open jeep or command car, directing, encouraging, and cajoling his soldiers in sub-zero temperatures. As he pushed his army forward, he began taking pictures of dead Germans again, something he hadn't done since Sicily. For all the action the Third Army saw, however, Patton's personal pictures during this period were extremely tame. He took a number of shots of open terrain, showing simple fences and tank ditches.

Two days after Patton's prediction of a German breakthrough, he awarded the members of this tank the Distinguished Service Cross for destroying four German tanks. The American tank knocked out the first two German tanks at 125 yards then charged the remaining two, destroying them at 50 yards. "Our tank had a track knocked off and several holes through it," Patton recorded, "but was not burned."[6]

On January 31, Patton's hard-driving ways caught up with him. He awoke in great pain, unable to see. His eyes had swollen shut from exposure and were "running like a spigot." A doctor applied cold compresses for two hours. Patton spent most of the day in bed. There would be no picture-taking that day.[5]

With Bastogne relieved and the Bulge eradicated, Patton found himself in front of cameras more often than behind them. On February 5, while planning his attack into Germany, he was summoned to Bastogne to meet Bradley and Eisenhower and to have his picture taken with his two commanders in the destroyed town.[7]

While the Battle of the Bulge showed Patton at his commanding best, his pictures for this stage of the war show his love for his troops and the conditions they had to endure to crush the final German offensive of the war.

A soldier takes Patton's picture in Saarlauten. The window of the wooden shed houses a machine gun portal. "Nearly all the houses I inspected," he confided, "are really forts."[8]

Patton's bridge across the Saar. Maj. Gen. Walton Walker wanted to walk across it with Patton, but Patton did not think it was worth the risk. His fears were unwarranted. "We had only one shot hit near us while doing so."[9]

Patton called these trenches "Chinese walls in reverse" and considered the amount of work that went into their excavation "appalling and to no purpose." [10]

(Above and Left) Patton attended Christmas mass at a church in Luxembourg City, where Kaiser Wilhelm had attended during World War I. An Army chaplain sent these pictures to Patton. [11]

PATTON PREPARES FOR THE BULGE

That Patton predicted the Battle of the Bulge has been well documented. What is less known is that he began preparing for the German offensive weeks before it was launched.

As early as November 25 Patton commented in his personal diary: "The First Army is making a terrible mistake leaving the VIII Corps static, as it is highly probable that the Germans are building up east of them."[10] This seeming footnote would remain in Patton's mind for the next twenty-one days, when the Wehrmacht fulfilled his prediction.

This prediction has been immortalized in biographies of the General, books on the Battle of the Bulge and the movie *Patton*. But Patton's insight to American unpreparedness and predictions of a German offensive were more complex than that single sentence. He kept an eye on the events north of his Third Army and slowly prepared for the eventuality of the Ardennes Offensive.

Six days earlier Patton was thinking of the VIII Corps' problems when he wrote to his wife about the inactivity of Lt. Gen. Courtney Hodges's First Army. "Courtney and Charley [Hodges's Chief of Staff] are doing nothing except fight the weather."[2] Patton saw the static First Army and was sure Hodges's inability to overcome the muddy terrain laid him open for a German attack. He concluded the letter by writing, "We beat the weather." Patton's way of dealing with any German counterattack was to keep his divisions moving forward, however slowly, and fighting, thus keeping the Wehrmacht off balance.

At the time of Patton's November 25 observation, the Germans were pouring men and material into the area west of the VIII Corps. He was occupied, however, with his own war. He busied himself with overseeing his division attacks, checking on supplies, visiting his divisions, worrying about replacements, receiving dignitaries and relieving

Patton was quite mobile during the Battle of the Bulge. Here he awaits his driver in his specialized jeep outside of General Eddy's headquarters. Patton titled this picture, "Bird in a Gilded Cage."[3]

one of his most valued division commanders, Maj. Gen. "P" Wood, the leader of the 4th Armored Division, who constantly clashed with his Corps commander, Manton Eddy.

On December 9, he placed both the 4th Armored Division and the 80th Infantry Division in reserve, resting them for future events. Patton began visiting his Corps and Division headquarters with the German offensive in mind. He wanted to make sure his men were ready for anything. On December 12, he visited the units of the XII Corps. At the 4th Armored Division, still in reserve, he visited two combat commands and checked out the men's food and shelter acquisitions. He rode into Domnom les Dieuze, where the 8th Tank Battalion was bedded down, standing in his jeep with full sirens blasting. In the town, he jumped out of the jeep and was greeted by Lt. Col. Albin Irzyk, who would always remember the visit. "He stopped at every cluster of soldiers and had something to say to each—a question, a word of encouragement or appreciation, a compliment, a wisecrack, a good-natured dig. In thirty minutes or so, he had touched every man in the battalion.[4] He tapped me on the

(CONTINUED)

On the march to Bastogne, Patton crossed the Sure River over a bridge like this one. He had to jump over the bodies of dead Americans as the bridge had no rails. The river was one of the biggest natural obstacles between the Third Army and the town.[12]

— PATTON PREPARES *(CONTINUED)*

back and said, 'You're doing a great job. Keep up the good work,'" Irzyk remembered. "Ironically, four days later it was my battalion that led the march to Bastogne."

Satisfied with the condition of his tankers, he next visited the 26th and 87th infantry divisions, since the 87th was replacing the 26th at the front. Last, he drove off to the 35th Division and saw how worn out the division was. When he returned to Third Army Headquarters, he decided to transform the 6th Armored and 26th Infantry Division into the III Corps. Positive that the Germans were about to strike the VIII, Patton wrote in his diary: "If the enemy attacks the VIII Corps of the First Army, as is probable, I can use III Corps to help."[5]

His plan to deal with any German surprise complete, he turned to his own impending attack. He planned to hit the German line on December 19, after a heavy air bombardment. His own feelings of success were limited, as he knew his men would run up against the formidable Siegfried Line. But even in the mayhem of planning his new offensive, events to the north kept nagging Patton's sixth sense. On December 13, he wrote to Beatrice,

"There is something in the 'air' which you will hear of long before you get this." Was he writing about his own offensive or the Germans? No one will ever know. It was three days before the Bulge.

On the eve of the German campaign, while Patton was strengthening his northern shoulder, Omar Bradley, the 12th Army Group commander, was weakening the First Army's front. Taking a "calculated risk," Bradley replaced the battle hardened and weary 2nd Infantry Division with the green 106th. Thus, Hitler's strongest attack in the West would hit the Allies at their weakest point.

But Patton was ready. In the time since his November 25 prediction, his army continued to advance and kept control of the battlefield. His army had also changed its shape from a center-heavy army in November to a more even army with a strong armor and infantry reserve, ready for action.

When Bradley called Patton late on December 16 and ordered him to move his 10th Armored Division north to aid in relieving the Bulge, Patton protested. But when he hung up the phone, he turned to Charles Codman and said, "I guess they're having trouble up there. I thought they would." Patton was ready for the Battle of the Bulge. ●

Patton got this picture from the gun camera of a P-47 Thunderbolt attack airplane. It was strafing a German column near Bastogne on Christmas day.[13]

For Christmas, Patton distributed prayer cards among the men of the Third Army. He ordered all chaplains to pray for dry weather. Patton credited his prayer for the three days of clear skies that followed, which helped him to relieve Bastogne. [14]

(Below) The Third Army pushes its way towards Bastogne by combining speed and firepower. Patton took this picture on Christmas night, calling it "Xmas greetings from the long toms."[15]

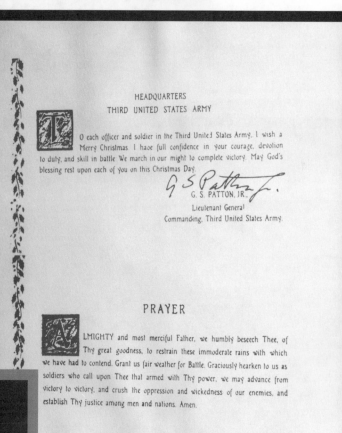

HEADQUARTERS
THIRD UNITED STATES ARMY

To each officer and soldier in the Third United States Army, I wish a Merry Christmas. I have full confidence in your courage, devotion to duty, and skill in battle. We march in our might to complete victory. May God's blessing rest upon each of you on this Christmas Day.

G. S. Patton, Jr.

G. S. PATTON, JR.
Lieutenant General
Commanding, Third United States Army.

PRAYER

ALMIGHTY and most merciful Father, we humbly beseech Thee, of Thy great goodness, to restrain these immoderate rains with which we have had to contend. Grant us fair weather for Battle. Graciously hearken to us as soldiers who call upon Thee that armed with Thy power, we may advance from victory to victory, and crush the oppression and wickedness of our enemies, and establish Thy justice among men and nations. Amen.

——— Mapping the Way to BASTOGNE ———

To supplement his albums, Patton sent his wife detailed maps showing his relief of Bastogne.

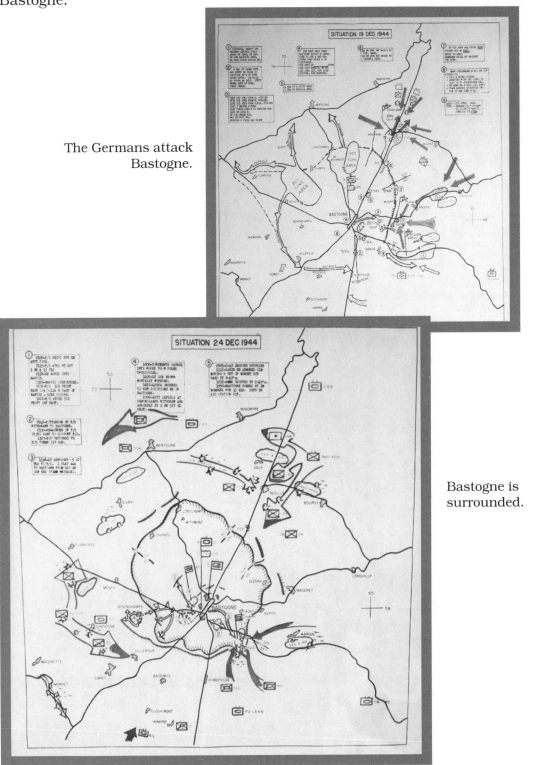

The Germans attack Bastogne.

Bastogne is surrounded.

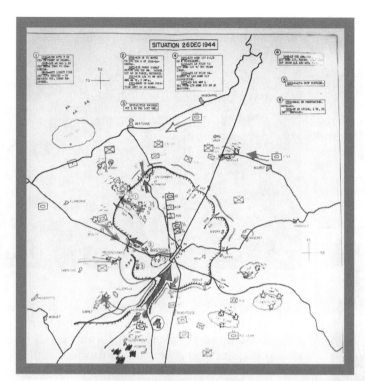

Bastogne is relieved by elements of the Third Army from the south, while German conterattacks continue in the west.

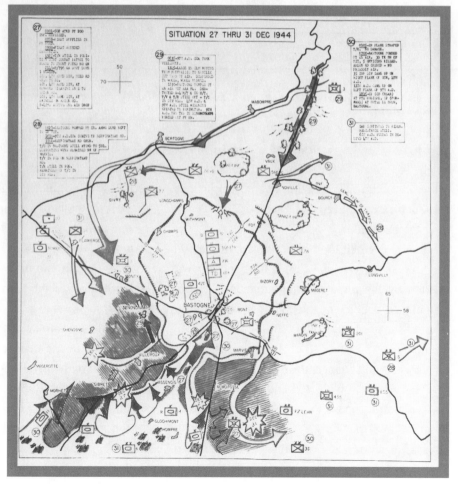

With Bastogne relieved, German forces try unsuccessfully to cut off the lifeline from the south.

Bastogne relieved! Patton took this picture in March, while flying to one of his corps headquarters. With a link established between Patton's men and the soldiers defending the town, Patton entered on December 30 to present medals and visit the men. "They were delighted and wanted me to drive slowly so the soldiers could see me." [16]

Maj. Gen. Hugh Gaffey congratulates Lt. James Fields of the 4th Armored Division on receiving the Medal of Honor. Fields knocked out two German gun positions and rescued a wounded soldier despite being wounded himself at the town of Rechicourt, France, back in September.

— TWO VERSIONS OF A PATTON TALE —

Patton always put himself in the best light in his diary entries and letters. He tended to go into great detail when describing his successes and skim over mistakes or embarrassments. One such case occurred on December 2, while visiting the front lines.

Patton decided to visit a regiment of the 90th Infantry Division along the Saar River. He was greeted by the regimental commander, Lt. Col. Raymond E. Bell, who guided him to the front and pointed out an enemy pillbox some 250 yards from their exposed position. "I felt conspicuous but fortunately nothing happened," he recorded in his diary. He then went with Bell and two members of his staff into a house that was being used as an observation post. "I always hate to go in OPs in houses," he continued, "as they are too conspicu-

ous and you always have a feeling that you are going to fall a long way from the roof, where the OP is situated. I was glad to leave, but feel that the Germans are not in Merzig or I would be dead."

Bell remembered the incident differently. According to him, the house was not an obvious target to the Germans since it was one of several and to get to it, Bell and his soldiers did not take the road, but approached it through an orchard next to the road, so as not to be spotted by the enemy. Bell offered the same route to Patton, but the General, resplendent in his distinctive uniform, refused. "Patton insisted on walking down the road which, in full view of the enemy, ran right by the house containing the observation post."

Bell, not yet a colonel and only a month into his new command, thought better than to argue with

(Left) Patton supplemented his photos to Beatrice with Army Signal Corps pictures. Here, an ordnance company of an armored division repairs vehicles. Note the editing crop marks.[17] (Right) A winterscape of Belgium. Patton considered the snow and terrain "a greater menace than the enemy." Temperatures through the end of December and into January were often below zero. Spring thaws would expose dead bodies and land mines. "It is amazing that men can exist, much less fight, in such weather."[18]

his renowned commander's logic. So the small party walked down the road, into the house, and up the stairs for a look at the enemy positions. Bell held his breath the whole way. "Sure enough," Bell recalled, "no sooner were we standing by the observers than the Germans opened up. I don't know where the rounds landed, but it did not matter. The rush down the stairs was a stampede. We managed to get out the back door of the house and then beat a very hasty retreat back to where the vehicles were parked in the orchard."

With German gunfire ripping through the air, everyone ran, including Patton, not up the exposed road this time but through the muddy orchard to reach safety. "By the time we arrived at the rendezvous point, Patton and his entourage were splattered with mud," Bell remembered. "The immacu-

lately clad General Patton, who had walked down the road to the observation post in full view of the Germans, now looked like he had spent a day in the trenches. I had to laugh, but not too loud."

Bell later concluded that Patton's chosen route had been his undoing. In full view of the Germans, and with a cluster of officers with him, not to mention his dress, which betrayed his rank and position, he offered an obvious target. It did not help that visibility that day was very clear, giving both sides a perfect view of each other.

It was not the first time Patton would downplay an event that showed him as a less-than-brilliant commander. But the incident showed that Patton was willing to visit the front and expose himself to the enemy. And he showed the front line soldiers that he was just as susceptible to enemy fire as they. ●

Patton visited St.Vith, the first major town taken by the Germans during the Battle of the Bulge. Patton compared it to the towns he saw in World War I. The Germans caused some of the destruction, but the Army Air Forces caused most of it, continually bombing the vital strategic crossroads until the Germans withdrew. "This was a city," he wrote on the picture.

Third Army soldiers stand next to a German tank that was hit twice by point-blank fire from an American halftrack. The dead crew was still in the tank when Patton took this picture.

This German machine gunner was killed within ten yards of a 94th Infantry Division outpost in Tuttlingen, Germany, in January 1945.

On January 22, 1945, Patton wrote to Beatrice that he "saw a lot of dead Germans yesterday frozen in funny attitudes. I got some good pictures but did not have my color camera, which was a pity, as they were a pale claret color." Patton's finger can be seen in the bottom left of the frame.[19]

VII
GERMANY

North Africa, Sicily, France, Belgium, and Luxembourg—Patton had helped drive the Germans out of all of them. Now came the prize: Germany. The campaigns into the Nazi heartland began in February and would not stop, save for a river to cross, until May. As always, Patton stayed close to the front, visiting troops and crossing bridges, sometimes the same day they were completed. His interest in enemy defenses and ancient ruins remained strong and his camera caught it all.

Patton entered Germany on February 13, 1945, over the Sauer River. He crossed in typical Patton style: American mortars coughing at the German lines, a smokescreen shielding him from enemy artillery spotters, and shells falling all around. Once across, he toured the Siegfried Line, Germany's last man-made defense. He thought some of the structures were "fantastic in their efficiency" but built by "gullible fools" who thought fixed fortifications could stop determined men.[1]

In Germany, Patton indulged himself in his love of history. He toured a number of castles, most of which he spotted from the air. When he flew to a corps headquarters, he passed over Bastogne, "getting some good pictures on the way."[2] Venturing deeper into Germany, Patton witnessed the destruction of the Germans and the power of the Third Army, driving through miles of wrecked enemy vehicles that had fallen victim to his tanks.

On the night of March 22, the Third Army crossed the last major barrier into the heart of Germany: the Rhine River. Most importantly for Patton, it was done before

Field Marshal Montgomery's meticulously prepared crossing to the north. For Patton, this was his own culmination of a great military career. He savored every moment and reenacted historical scenes to add drama to his accomplishment. Halfway across the river, he got out of his command jeep, opened his fly, and relieved himself in the river. Every soldier in the area with a camera snapped away while the General enjoyed himself. On the opposite bank he fell to the ground, grabbed two handfuls of dirt and got up, saying, "Thus, William the Conqueror." Patton, demonstrating his knowledge of history, emulated William's fall while disembarking from a boat on England's shore. William is said to have exclaimed, "I have taken England with both hands!"[3]

With the Rhine breached, German defenses began to crumble. While strong areas of resistance remained, more and more soldiers surrendered. Every time a new milestone was reached, the last prisoner was photographed with a sign celebrating the number of the latest surrender.

Into Germany! When Patton visited these engineers building a bridge across the Sauer River into Germany, he remarked that he had never seen so many small men in his life, inspiring the sign. The area was still under artillery fire when Patton took this picture.[4]

Patton's performance since arriving in France had been spectacular, but once in Germany he took a risk that defied military logic and good sense. On the chance that his son-in-law, John Waters, who had been captured in North Africa, was in a POW camp in Hammelburg, Patton sent an armored task force behind enemy lines to liberate the camp and rescue Waters. On March 26 the armored force punched through the German line and raced for Hammelburg. Included among the liberators was Patton's aide, Maj. Al Stiller, who could identify Waters in the confusion. During the assault on the camp, Waters was shot and wounded. GI prisoners were loaded onto vehicles for the return to American lines, but the task force ran into a German trap and, after a fierce firefight, was forced to surrender. Waters remained in the camp for another week until liberated by units of the Seventh Army. Stiller remained a prisoner even longer, forcing Patton to make Francis Graves, another son of Patton's friends in California, his new aide.[5] Patton was overjoyed a few days later when

Waters was found in good condition. Patton had his gaunt son-in-law flown to a hospital in Frankfurt where he visited him and took his picture. Waters eventually rose to the rank of four-star general.

As the Third Army pushed deeper into Germany, Patton continued his practice of flying between corps headquarters. On one occasion a Spitfire pilot mistook Patton's Piper Cub for a German Fieseler Storch and strafed it three times. Patton, wanting to "take some pictures of my impending demise," took out his camera and photographed the action. Unfortunately, "I found that I had been so nervous I had forgotten to take the cover off the lens and all I got were blanks."[6]

The war was winding down. In the last days of April, the Third Army crossed the Danube River in four places. Patton crossed on a treadway bridge and took pictures of the river and a barge carrying a U-boat in pieces. He flew over Nuremberg and Regensburg and took pictures of the destroyed cities. As he neared Regensburg he reiterated his belief in reincarnation and reminded his aide, Colonel Codman, that he had stormed the city as a soldier in Napoleon's army.

In the last few days of the war Patton took up residence in the palace of the Prince of Thurn und Taxis in Regensburg, a castle that dated back to the 1700s. He was overwhelmed by the castle's amenities and icy-cold temperatures. With little else to do—Patton now considered the war dull—he began enjoying himself. He posed for pictures in Valhalla, the temple of tribute to the great men of German history. Even Willie got a seat at the memorial. Aides got into the spirit too: Graves dressed up in German garb for Patton to record.

On May 1, Patton entered a POW camp in Moosburg to the cheers of the prisoners. As he greeted the men the cameras clicked, but Patton would not see the pictures for months.[7] Eight days later the war in Europe ended. The Third Army had reached Czechoslovakia and Patton was in Pilsen, taking pictures of German tanks and armored vehicles to send home for study.

The war was over, and the campaign into Germany had proved all of Patton's training and passion. His camera caught more action in Germany than in any other campaign, and he used fewer Signal Corps photos than ever. Patton had helped end the war but was not looking forward to the peace. "I love the war and responsibility and excitement. Peace is going to be hell on me." The rest of 1945 would prove how right he was.[8]

Patton tours the west bank of the Rhine River while vehicles of the Third Army drive in to Germany.

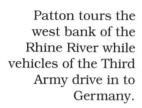

After crossing the bridge, Patton examined this German pillbox, which had withstood direct hits from a 90 mm cannon and a bazooka, but, he wrote, "none ever penetrated." Despite the strength of the turret, Patton considered such obstacles not worth a damn. "We got one direct hit in the embrasure, which cleaned it out."[9]

Near Bitburg, Patton saw these dragon's teeth, cement pylons laid out to block tanks and other vehicles. He considered them "a useless form of amusement."[10]

Tank tracks from the air.

With the war going well, Patton had time to indulge his interest in history. He visited the Château de Bourscheid, whose previous owner was Prince Metternich. Patton spotted the castle from the air.[11]

A bridge over the Saar near Trier. The bridge to the right was blown up by the Germans to deny it to the Third Army. General Bradley sent Patton a message telling him to bypass Trier, since it would take four divisions to capture it. Patton sent this response to his superior: "Have taken Trier with two divisions. What do you want me to do? Give it back?"[12]

In mid-February, with the Bulge closed and the front somewhat static, Patton took a few days' leave in Paris, where he ordered this flatware with the Third Army insignia on it. The set arrived in mid-March, "I paid for it personally." It cost him $300.[13]

Someone lost a bet. A captain with the Fifteenth Army poses with Lt. Gen. William H. Simpson, the commander of the Ninth Army at an award ceremony. While Simpson was easily recognizable by his bald head, the captain's has obviously been shaved. While the captain is not identified, Maj. Chet Hansen, an aide to Gen. Omar Bradley, included a message with the photo that read: "Dear Charlie [Codman], Simply to warn you that the General [Simpson]'s impulses can lead to things like this."

Death and Destruction near NEUSTADT

As Patton drove near the town of Neustadt, he saw "one of the greatest scenes of destruction I have ever witnessed." American tanks had collided with a German column and tore into it. For two miles, wrecked German vehicles and, "I am sorry to say, dead horses" littered the road.

American tanks drove straight down this column of German vehicles, forcing them into the gully. "A tanker's dream come true," Patton cheered.

The tanks fired into these cars from as little as ten feet away.

(Below) Patton noticed that there were no dead Germans among the wreckage. He assumed they had already been buried.

Engineers build a bridge over the Rhine River. Patton crossed it a day before his rival, Montgomery. He wrote a quote from Secretary of War Henry Stimson on the back of the photo: "We gave Monty everything he asked for—paratroops, assault boats, and even the Navy, and by God! Patton has crossed the Rhine!"

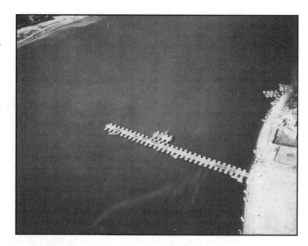

Patton stands midway on his Rhine River bridge. Seconds later he urinated into the river. "The pause that refreshes," he called it. Though pictures of the 'christening' were taken, Patton did not send one to his wife. (See page 4)

(Below) Another aerial view of the Rhine shows a railway bridge and a pontoon bridge below a knocked-out bridge. Patton wrote "anti mine net" to point out the protection two days after his crossing.[14]

The Third Army processes the 500,000th prisoner of war taken after August 1, a thousand more than the First Army, which had a two-month start on the war. By this point in the war, he knew the German army was spent. "I do not see how they can keep it up much longer," Patton confided.[15]

Among Patton's prisoners were high-ranking Nazi officials. Walter Scheiber, seen here sitting between Hitler and Rudolf Hess, became a prisoner of the Third Army. Scheiber was the head of the supply department in Albert Speer's production ministry. Patton compared him to Donald Nelson, President Roosevelt's head of the War Production Board.[16]

A gaunt Col. John Waters looks up from his hospital bed in Frankfurt. Once the Seventh Army captured his POW camp in early April, Patton had him flown to an Army hospital, where he took this picture. Within one day of treatment Patton noticed that Waters "is much better, having a blood transfusion and a hot meal consisting of chicken and potatoes." The next day, Patton concluded: "His spirit is unbroken and he is in fine shape."[17]

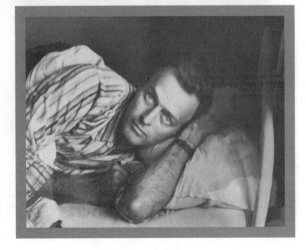

(Left) Presidential advisor Bernard Baruch visits Patton at his headquarters. Patton later accused him of being too critical of Nazi atrocities against Jews and other minorities in Germany. Patton saw Baruch and others who were bringing to light the horrors of the Holocaust as merely out for "Semetic [sic] revenge." (Below) In the last days of April, Patton crossed the Danube River on this bridge as the Third Army moved toward Czechoslovakia. He was not impressed with the river, though he considered it quite swift.[18]

While crossing, Patton saw a German barge with an entire U-boat on board in sections. In the background is "some kind of Nazi shrine which I did not have a chance to investigate." He would later find out it was Valhalla.[19]

PLANES OVER HAMMELBURG

From the day Patton's son-in-law, Lt. Col. John Waters—husband of his oldest daughter "Little Bee"—was captured by the Germans in the Tunisian desert, he was always in the back of Patton's mind. The general waited for over a month after Waters' capture, not knowing if he was a live prisoner or a dead soldier. He was greatly relieved when a German transmission confirmed that Waters was in German hands.[1]

After that, Waters name would pop up every so often in Patton's diary. He would ask Beatrice if Little Bee had heard from John, and relayed anything he found out on Waters' location. It should be no surprise, therefore, that when the Third Army neared the POW camp Waters was suspected to be in, Patton wanted to do something bold to rescue him. It was a bad idea.

Instead of sending the 4th Armored Division, or even a combat command composed of around 4,000 men and 150 tanks, Patton insisted on sending a small task force, headed by Capt. Abe Baum, composed of 307 men with 10 medium tanks, 6 light tanks, 27 half-tracks, 7 jeeps, 3 motorized assault guns, and one cargo carrier. The mission was to break through the German lines and charge for the Hammelburg POW camp some forty miles away. Patton sent his assistant, Maj. Al Stiller, to accompany Baum, since Stiller could recognize Waters. On top of sending too small a force, Patton provided no air cover for the mission.

The raid was a disaster. Launched in the early morning darkness of March 26, 1945, Baum and his men made it to the camp but lost vehicles along the way. Once they arrived at the camp, Waters was shot while organizing the mostly peaceful surrender of the camp. Baum was told to expect 300 Americans, but when his tanks crashed through the camp gate they discovered 5,000 men in the camp, of which 1,500 were Americans. He put as many

Americans onto his vehicles as possible. Waters, because of his wound, would have to stay behind. But German resistance grew and Baum decided to try to break out the next morning. Unbeknownst to him, the Germans spent the night surrounding his position. At first light, before Baum could execute his plan, the Germans opened up on his survivors. Baum was forced to surrender.[2]

Would air cover have made a difference? According to Baum: not in the beginning stages of the raid. "We relied on an artillery plane for air cover and thought it would radio in for us to get the air cover, but an L4 [observation plane] could only go so far. In addition, we were moving too fast." Fighters and bombers, so vital to troops preparing to attack a position, were practically useless to fast-moving vehicles. While they might have made a difference in slowing German reinforcements trying to reach the task force, since Patton knew exactly where they were headed, it was too risky to have them engage any Germans dueling with Baum's tanks.[3]

But once the task force reached the POW camp and continued fighting the ever-growing German presence, P-47s and P-51s could have made a big difference. "I could have used air power," Baum confessed, "but even there it would have been difficult."

The last opportunity where planes could have made a difference was the second and final day of the raid, when Baum's surviving men and vehicles were surrounded and pounded by the Germans. "It would have made a difference if we knew where the enemy was." Baum had spent the night not thinking about air cover but siphoning fuel from damaged vehicles and putting it into those that still ran. At dawn the Germans attacked swiftly and violently. Baum would not have had the time to call in an air strike even if the air assets were at hand. "As

(CONTINUED)

Patton considered Nuremberg "pathetic and all blown to hell." He deemed it the most destroyed place he had ever seen. He thought it a shame "to see such a historical monument so completely removed."[20]

— PLANES OVER HAMMELBURG *(CONTINUED)* —

far as I was concerned, it would have been too long." Baum explained that air planes need a mission and they did not have one for his raid, but shouldn't Patton have ordered a mission instead of keeping the raid a secret?

Patton obviously wanted few people to know what he was up to in case things turned out the way they did. He had to know the raid would stir up a hornet's nest, yet he failed to assign a ground controller to the force in case of an emergency.[4] He knew the mission was risky, and he made it worse by depriving Baum's men of tools to guarantee success. Patton, who had almost been sent home for slapping two soldiers, and for revealing his presence in England before D-Day, was left alone after sacrificing 307 men on a rash and personal quest.

Baum confronted Patton in early April, when Patton came to Baum's hospital to visit Waters, recovering on a different floor. Patton eventually came down to pin a medal on Baum for his bravery in the failed raid. Baum asked him if the mission was to retrieve a single man and Patton told him it was not. Baum wondered if Patton would be court-martialed but decided he would have no part in it. "I wasn't gonna rock the boat," Baum explained. "He was one of our greatest generals and he ended the war 6 or 8 months earlier than it would have lasted." Baum was also relieved to find out his small raid had distracted the Germans from a larger attack further north by the rest of the 4th Armored Division. Despite Baum's forgiveness, Hammelburg remains the one military stain on Patton's record. The camp's liberation was an eventuality, and the soldiers were protected by the Geneva Convention and were not in danger of mass executions like the prisoners of Japan. But Patton, nervous about his son-in-law's well being, broke with his military logic and maxims and tried for a Hail Mary play, risking too much in the process. ●

As Patton neared the city of Regensburg (also known as Ratisbon) with his aide, Codman, he harkened back to one of his "previous lives," saying, "You know, we French stormed Ratisbon. On a little mound, Napoleon stood on our storming day." Patton strongly believed in reincarnation.[21]

The American POW camp in Regensburg held 50,000 prisoners. The city was the last the Third Army occupied. Shell craters can be seen in the lower left.[22]

Patton moved his headquarters to the palace of the Prince of Thurn und Taxis in Regensburg. He did not like his accommodations, and thought the castle "cold as hell, that is why my writing is so poor. I am shaking with cold and so is Willie." He eventually resorted to sleeping in his mobile headquarters.[23]

The rooms of the palace were adorned with hunting trophies, suits of armor and portraits. "I saw it yesterday and have never beheld so much gaudy junk [in] each room," he wrote to Beatrice. "There were [sic] at least a hundred and three times too much stuff in it."[24]

To celebrate his victory, Patton posed for pictures in Valhalla, a memorial to famous Germans built in the early 1800s by King Ludwig. Patton is wearing his new four-star rank.[25]

Willie also earned a seat at the famed memorial.[28]

A German assassin? Not really. The soldier is Francis Graves, in a German uniform. Graves had become one of Patton's aides when Major Stiller was captured during the Hammelburg raid. Patton sent a copy of the picture to Graves's parents, who were friends of his from California.[27]

Patton greets Major Stiller upon his release from a German POW camp on April 29. Stiller had lost thirty pounds after almost a month in captivity.[28]

On the first of May, Patton visited Stalag VIIA in Moosburg, where prisoners from Hammelburg had been marched. Patton thought there were too many prisoners in the camp. They gave him "quite an ovation." To Beatrice this photo was special. He mailed it to her on the day of his fatal car accident on December 9, 1945. [29]

Beatrice appreciated her husband's last mailing. She put the envelope in the album collection with its postage stamp clearly visible.

The Third Army holds its last briefing of the war in Europe. Patton thanked his staff for the work they had done to win the war and added, "I hope we will have other, similar briefings in China."[30]

The last day of the war found Patton in Pilsen, Czechoslovakia, taking pictures at the bombed-out Skoda Munitions Plant. Ever the consummate tanker, he discovered in the rubble "a new form of bogie suspension for the tanks, of which I took some pictures. I believe that for light tanks it is very satisfactory."

PATTON'S POETRY

As early as his cadet days at West Point, Patton wrote poetry. He wrote for himself, his wife, and the public, and though his verses were rarely published, they can be found in a number of his biographies.

Some poems, such as "Through a Glass Darkly," which was used in the movie *Patton*, are well-known to Patton scholars. Others have been forgotten. Many were deemed too vulgar for the reading public. One poem Patton wrote, and had his young daughter memorize, resulted in her being sent to the principal's office.

In early March 1945, Beatrice sent this poem to *Colliers,* a national weekly magazine, for publication. The poem was rejected rather bluntly. The magazine's editor explained to Beatrice that the editors "are of the opinion that nothing more should be printed that will revive the 'Old Blood and Guts' legend." Even though the war was still raging and Patton at this point in the war was synonymous with victory, his poem about combat was too severe for the people at home. It was never published. ●

Song of the Bayonet

From the hot furnace, throbbing with passion
First was I stamped in the form to destroy.
And the fierce heat of my birth has removed
Out of my heart every wish but one joy.

Carefully tempered was I, and well sharpened
Ever and always pursuing my trust.
How have I yearned as we rushed
on the dummies
For the hot draft at the end of the thrust.

Deep in the faggots and sacks have I burrowed
Seeking still vainly to slake my long thirst.
Gouging and prodding the dummies with venom
Viciously, stubbornly doing my worst.

Then on a morning, wet and o'er-clouded
Was my long hunger sated at last.
Deep in his entrails the short lunge had sent me,
Rich was the blood of my final repast.

VIII
POSTWAR

The war was over. Patton, the leader of one of the greatest armies in history, settled down to become the military governor of Bavaria. He was poorly suited for the job and did not enjoy it, choosing instead to spend his time attending victory parades, hunting, and reviewing troops. His photographs took on a more historic and ceremonial nature, as they had during his idle times in North Africa and Sicily. He began collecting huge stacks of Army Signal Corps pictures of visiting dignitaries, awards ceremonies, and even his birthday party.

Patton's first order of business was to attend victory parades of the Allies. His hatred of the Russians was already well developed. Ten days after the war, he sent his wife a number of pictures of "me and the Mongols."[1] More public statements disagreeing with Eisenhower's policies in occupied Germany would eventually cost him his command.

Patton took up residence in Bad Tölz, a former Nazi Youth complex, to rule the area. He wasn't there long before returning to the United States on June 7, 1945, to a hero's welcome. Along the way he photographed his bomber escort across the Atlantic. Landing in Boston, it was his turn again to be photographed—hugging his wife. He attended victory parades and delivered speeches selling war bonds to finance the war in the Pacific, where he longed to be. After Boston he went to California, where he spoke at the Memorial Coliseum in Los Angeles along with his friend, Lt. Gen. Jimmy Doolittle. Before returning to Europe, he visited Fort Riley, Kansas, and Hamilton, Massachusetts, to give speeches, selling millions of dollars worth of war bonds in the process.[2]

Returning to Europe, Patton got himself into more trouble by keeping former Nazis in power, treating displaced persons—mostly Jews still in their concentration camps—

poorly, and, of course, for his statements about the Russians. He was relieved of the command of the Third Army and given command of the Fifteenth Army, an administrative unit assigned to write the "lessons learned" of the war in Europe.

Patton was still a celebrity. When he and Eisenhower attended a football game between army units, Eisenhower walked over to a balcony beneath which soldiers with cameras were being held back by military policeman. He was greeted with shouts of "We want General Patton!" and he went inside to and retrieve the general.[3] Patton was also popular in France, where he attended liberation celebrations in numerous towns and cities.[4]

He toured Copenhagen, Denmark, and Sweden, where he had competed in the Modern pentathlon at the 1912 Olympics. He met with the Swedish royal family, attended a hockey game, and competed with his old Olympic adversaries at a pistol shoot. He also visited several military installations. At one base, motorcycle troops put on a small precision drill for him. Patton pulled out his camera and snapped away.

These were the last pictures Patton ever took. Ten days later, he left his Bad Tölz headquarters to go on a hunting trip. Before departing, he mailed the pictures of himself at the Moosburg POW camp to his wife and got into his car. He did not get far. An Army truck hit his car near Mannheim and fatally injured him. Paralyzed from the neck down, he lingered for twelve days in a Heidelberg hospital before succumbing to a blood clot in his lung on December 21, 1945. The day after his death his belongings,

With the war over, Patton attends a victory parade with his Soviet counterpart. "We have met the Russians and they are ours," he wrote. After presenting the Russian commander with the Legion of Merit, Patton took him to the Officers' Club. "I unquestionably drank the Russian commander under the table and walked out under my own steam."[5]

including the camera, were packed up and shipped home to Massachusetts. When Beatrice received his effects she discovered the film in his camera and developed his last photos.

The Third Army Headquarters at Bad Tölz, a Nazi Youth complex.

The entrance to Third Army Headquarters.

Patton's residence at Bad Tölz. It had a bowling alley, a swimming pool, a large number of rooms, and a boathouse with two boats. "If one has to occupy Germany," Patton mused, "this is a good place to do it from."[6]

Gen. Hobart Gay stands in front of Patton's villa. Patton's window is on the second floor. He furnished his office with Rommel's desk, which had been discovered in Stuttgart.[7]

(Below) Patton's boat at Bad Tölz.

BERLIN IN RUINS

Patton toured Berlin, which he had visited in 1912 after participating in the Olympic Games. He considered the city "not nearly as much bashed-in as was reported," but the destruction depressed him. He decided the Allies had fought the wrong enemy. "We have destroyed what could have been a good race and are about to replace them with Mongolian savages."[8]

Patton stayed at the Adlon Hotel in 1912, near Berlin's famous Brandenburg Gate. The Gate was commissioned by Emperor Freidrich Wilhelm II to represent peace. Ironically, it became part of the Berlin Wall during the years of Communist rule.

Another view of the Adlon, from across the street, July 1945.

Patton took this picture of Berlin in ruins while standing on the steps of the Reichstag, the seat of the Bundestag, the German parliament.

The Reichstag was heavily damaged when the Soviets entered Berlin. In Patton's photograph, graffiti using the Cyrillic alphabet can be seen on the Reichstag's outer columns.

— THE PATTON COLLECTION

For anyone interested in leadership, military history or Patton himself, the Patton Collection at the Library of Congress is amazing.

Patton's papers were given to the Manuscripts Division of the Library of Congress in three different sets: first, in 1955 by Mrs. Samuel J. Graham; second, in 1964 by Patton's children, George S. Patton IV, Beatrice Waters, and Ruth Ellen Totten as well as John Waters, Patton's son-in-law, and George Patton Waters, Patton's grandson. A third batch was delivered by Martin Blumenson between 1970 and 1986.

The collection is rather eclectic. Along with personal notes from Dwight D. Eisenhower, George C. Marshall, President Roosevelt, and British Prime Minister Churchill, there is a document signed by Adolf Hitler. There's another piece of Hitler memorabilia in the collection. While in North Africa, Patton pulled a postcard with Hitler's picture on it off the body of a dead German. The soldier had kept it in his breast pocket and there is a perfectly symmetrical hole in the card where an American bullet penetrated the German.

Patton's diaries are in three forms: The originals which are in Patton's poor handwriting, typed transcripts that have been annotated by his wife, and microfilm of the typed transcripts. All of Patton's misspellings have been copied letter by letter onto the transcripts. His letters to Beatrice have also been transcribed and annotated by her. The annotations are invaluable as they provide brief biographies of people Patton mentions in passing or elaborate on some point Patton made.

Patton also kept any report he found useful. The collection is filled with after-action reports on the accidental shooting down of paratrooper planes during the invasion of Sicily, reports on the relief of Bastogne, and a rather enlightening study of African Americans in the military—equating their difficulties to their economic background, not the color of their skin.

All together, the collection, housed in the Library of Congress's Manuscripts Division, contains approximately 26,100 items in seventy-seven boxes, including the photo albums, scrap books, and maps. Everyone is welcome to explore the collection; all they need is a researcher's card. Unfortunately, the collection cannot be viewed in its entirety at one time. It is in a secure area and the only way to see anything in the collection is by picking items from an index file. But for the serious researcher, it's worth it. ●

A Lipizzan stallion. The horses were originally in Vienna, but the Germans brought them west as the Russians advanced on the city. Patton noted that they had been "running since the time of Charles V."

Patton's horse jumps over an obstacle. Although Patton was too old to play polo, he still rode for exercise.

Patton heads home. An escort of B-17 bombers flanks his plane as he approaches Boston. He later told a crowd that, as he flew over the United States, he saw no shell holes, destroyed bridges or roofless houses like he was used to in Europe. "It was all wrong!"[9]

(Above) Patton arrives at Bedford,
Massachusetts, for the first leg of his war
bond campaign.[10]

(Right) Patton greets Bea for the first
time since leaving for North Africa
three years earlier. Patton commented
that someone called it "the best
picture of the war."[11]

(Below) Patton's son, George IV, was on
hand in his West Point uniform to greet his
father in Boston.

Patton doffs his helmet to the one million people who jammed the 25-mile parade route leading to the Hatch Memorial Shell in Boston, where he delivered a war bonds speech. He told the audience that it was beneath his dignity to ask people to buy war bonds. "I tell you it is your duty!" he commanded.[12]

Patton did not get home until 1:30 A.M. when he and Beatrice posed for a quick photograph.

Patton delivers his speech at the Shell. When he addressed the crowd and mentioned that he weighed much less as a younger man, the crowd roared with laughter. "I resent that," he snapped. "My weight is due to more brains."[13]

Patton shakes hands with the mayor of Beverly, Massachusetts, Daniel E. McLean, believing this picture would be used to make a stamp. Patton drew the wreath on it.[14]

At the Memorial Coliseum in Los Angeles, California, Patton called the Japanese, "those indescribable . . . people." He also called himself and Gen. Jimmy Doolittle (third from the right) two "lucky old bums born in California."[15]

While he was in California, Patton gave a copy of Hitler's *Mein Kampf* to the Huntington Library as a gift.[16]

Patton spoke to a crowd at an American Legion post in Hamilton, a suburb of Boston. The review stand was built in the outfield of a baseball field. More than 4,500 people attended.[17]

Before returning to Europe, Patton went to Fort Riley, Kansas, his first post in the army, to visit some old friends. From left to right they are: Ernie Hammon, Patton's signal officer throughout the war; Col. James O'Neill, the chaplain for the Third Army; Col. Oscar Koch, Patton's intelligence officer throughout the war; Col. H. Ford; and Col. Robert Allen, Koch's assistant.

Patton returns to Germany after his tour of the United States.

The booty of war. Patton climbs out of Hermann Göring's personal train, which Patton claimed for himself. Göring, the head of the German Luftwaffe and second in command of Nazi Germany, surrounded himself with opulence. The train consisted of two 12-compartment sleeping cars, a dining car, and a car with a dressing room, a bathroom with a marble tub, and a bedroom.[18]

Wearing the shoulder patch of the Fifteenth Army, Patton cuts his birthday cake at a surprise party held at the Grand Hotel in the famous spa town of Bad Nauheim.[19]

GET WELL, GENERAL PATTON

When Patton's Cadillac collided with an oncoming Army truck at a railroad crossing outside of Mannheim on December 9, 1945, he was the only one injured. Sitting sideways in the back seat, he flew up into the air and smashed the top of his head into a clock and the steel frame of the car's partition. It tore the skin off the top of his head and cracked two of the vertebrae in his neck. "I think I'm paralyzed," he told a doctor who arrived on the scene before being rushed to a hospital in Heidelberg.

Days after the accident, cards and letters began arriving at Patton's hospital room. The first were from fellow generals and President Harry Truman. Soon, others followed from common soldiers and civilians back in the United States, mostly from those with a loved one in the military.

Beatrice, ever at Patton's side since she had arrived on December 11, picked out the cards or Western Union messages she thought her husband would appreciate and read them to him. She later pasted each one onto pages in a card book, eventually filling seven books.

Children as young as nine wrote to tell Patton they were praying for him. Parents wrote, too, telling the famous patient that they made sure their children, some as young as four, kept Patton in their prayers. One man wrote that he "prayed so doggon [sic] hard" for Patton's recovery. A man whose son fought in the Third Army told Patton that he did not pray often but started after he heard about the accident. Another man may have been nervous about writing Patton when he wrote "you have been an admirer of mine."

General Eisenhower visits Patton at Bad Tölz in mid-September. He was shocked to find that Patton had left SS soldiers in charge of security at concentration camps, and had done little to improve the conditions of displaced persons, particularly the Jews. The visit, as well as Patton's public statements that ran counter to Eisenhower's denazification policy, led to his dismissal as commander of the Third Army.

Some of the letters were a bit extreme. A woman who taught for fifty years harkened back to the Sicilian campaign when she told Patton that she admired him for everything he did and confessed that she often felt like slapping her students. A Mr. and Mrs. Dowell sent Patton a card offering their condolences and asking him to look into sending their son home from Europe in time for Christmas. They wrote that he had earned seventy points in the Army's system for return eligibility. Soldiers needed eighty-five points, gained through time overseas, campaigns, medals, and marriage, to be sent home.

As newspapers reported that Patton was recovering, a number of spinal injury survivors, mostly military men, wrote offering advice and hope. A Navy veteran told Patton he had suffered the exact same injury and was now walking. Another suggested that Patton find God in order to recover.

Unfortunately, the cards, prayers, and well-wishes were not enough to sustain the General. He succumbed to a blood clot in his lung, a common result of paralysis, on December 21. Five months earlier, when he had gone to the United States, he had told his family it would be the last time he would ever be home. He was right. Today Patton is buried at the American Military Cemetery at Hamm in Luxembourg at the head of his men lying under crosses and stars of David.[1] He was originally buried among his men, but so many people came to visit his grave that his body had to be moved to a more convenient location. ●

(Left) Patton takes a salute from a soldier in Metz. He visited the French city in November to return the local cathedral's treasure, which he had captured in Germany. The citizens of Metz, grateful for Patton's liberation of their town in 1944, made him a Citizen of Honor. Patton, for his part, boasted that, before him, the town had not been taken by assault since Attila the Hun. He added that one of his officers commented that, when Patton received a Silver Star for the town's capture, "Never was so little given for so much."[20] (Right) He also was made an honorary citizen of Chartres.

PATTON'S LAST PHOTOS

These are the last pictures Patton ever took. On December 1, while visiting Sweden, he watched a precision motorcycle team perform, riding at 40 miles per hour on icy roads. Ten days later he was fatally injured in a car accident. It was not until Beatrice received his effects after his death that she discovered the film in the camera and developed his final shots.[21]

NOTES

Chapter 1: The General and His Hobby

1. Allen, *Lucky Forward*, 381.
2. Item Catalog Sheet No. 27.48.00, Patton Museum of Cavalry and Armor, Fort Knox, Kentucky.
3. George S. Patton [GSP] to Beatrice A. Patton [BAP], 8 September 1944, Box 18, Folder 8, George S. Patton Collection, Manuscripts Division, Library of Congress.
4. GSP to BAP, 2 July 1943, Box 19, Folder 14.

Chapter 2: North Africa

1. GSP to Gen. George Marshall [GM], 15 November 1942, Box 32, Folder M.
2. GSP to BAP, 14 November 1942, Box 19, Folder 9.
3. GSP to BAP, 5 December 1942, Box 19, Folder 10.
4. GSP to BAP, 27 November 1942, Box 19, Folder 9; GSP to Fred Ayer [FA], 27 January 1943, Box 19, Folder 10.
5. Blumenson, *The Patton Papers, 1940–1945*, 193.
6. Oversized [OV] 12, 3, George S. Patton Collection, Manuscripts Division, Library of Congress.
7. OV 12, 12.
8. OV 12, 8; GSP to GM, 15 November 1942, Box 32, Folder M.
9. OV 14, 7.
10. Atkinson, *An Army at Dawn*, 459.
11. GSP to BAP, 17 April 1943, Box 19, Folder 12.
12. GSP to BAP, 24 May 1943, Box 19, Folder 13.
13. OV 12, 12; Blumenson, *The Patton Papers, 1940–1945*, 110.
14. OV 12, 16.
15. OV 12, 52.
16. Blumenson, *The Patton Papers, 1940–1945*, 140.
17. Blumenson, *The Patton Papers, 1940–1945*, 125.
18. Blumenson, *The Patton Papers, 1940–1945*, 140.
19. OV 13, 24; GSP to BAP, 12 December 1942, Box 19, Folder 13.
20. OV 13, 24; GSP to BAP, 12 December 1942, Box 19, Folder 13.
21. Patton's diaries, 21 January 1943, Box 2, Folder 13, George S. Patton Collection, Manuscripts Division, Library of Congress.
22. OV 12, 30; GSP to BAP, 3 February 1943, Box 19, Folder 11; GSP to FA, 18 January 1943, Box 14, Folder 14; Patton's diaries, 2 February 1943, Box 2, Folder 14.
23. Patton's diaries, 12 March 1943, Box 2, Folder 14.
24. OV 14, 12; GSP to George Patton IV [GP IV], 7 April 1943, Box 21, Folder 3.
25. OV 14, 13.
26. Blumenson, *The Patton Papers, 1940–1945*, 198.

27. OV 12, 60.
28. Blumenson, *The Patton Papers, 1940–1945*, 203 and 221.
29. Atkinson, *An Army at Dawn*, 485.
30. Mercer, *Chronicle of the World,* 191 and 193; Blumenson, *The Patton Papers 1940–1945,* 221; OV 14, 17.
31. OV 13, 35.
32. Blumenson, *The Patton Papers, 1940–1945,* 225.

Patton's Beatrice

1. Totten, *The Button Box; A Daughter's Loving Memoir of Mrs. George S. Patton* (Columbia: The University of Missouri Press), 195, 300, 369, 373.
2. Totten, *The Button Box,* 95.
3. Totten, *The Button Box,* 331.
4. Beatrice to Patton, 1 April 1943, Box 19, Folder 11.
5. Interview, Gen. Walter T. Kerwin.
6. D'Este, *Patton: A Genius for War* (New York: HarperCollins), 806-807.

Chapter 3: Sicily

1. OV 13, 57.
2. OV 16, 66.
3. OV 13, 52.
4. OV 13, 62.
5. OV 13, 69; GP IV to Patton Museum, 30 October 1972, Patton Museum of Cavalry and Armor, Fort Knox, Kentucky.
6. OV 15, 2; Blumenson, *The Patton Papers 1940–1942,* 286.
7. OV 15, 10.
8. OV 15, p 10 and 11; Blumenson, *The Patton Papers, 1940–1945,* 295.
9. OV 15, 11.
10. Blumenson, *The Patton Papers, 1940–1945,* 295.
11. OV 13, 71; Patton's diaries, 23 June, 1943, Box 3, Folder 1.
12. OV 16, 6; Patton's diaries, 19 June 1943, Box 3, Folder 1.

13. OV 13, 71; Patton's diaries, 25 June 1943, Box 3, Folder 2.
14. Blumenson, *The Patton Papers, 1940–1945,* 321.
15. OV 13, 70.
16. OV 15, 1.
17. Phillips, *The Making of a Professional: Manton S. Eddy, USA,* 5.
18. Phillips, *The Making of a Professional: Manton S. Eddy, USA,* 122.
19. GSP to Paddy Flint, 12 June 1944, Box 29, Folder 17.
20. "Keeping Faith: A Tribute to Col. Harry Albert Flint," Box 52, Folder 12; and Phillips, *The Making of a Professional: Manton S. Eddy, USA,* 147.
21. "Keeping Faith," Box 52, Folder 12; GSP to Sallie Flint, 13 July 1944, Box 29, Folder 13; and D'Este, *Patton: A Genius For War,* 741.
22. OV 15, 2; Patton's diaries, 12 August 1943, Box 3, Folder 2.
23. OV 15, 12 and 13.
24. OV 15, 20; Blumenson, *The Patton Papers, 1940–1945,* 324.

Disaster in the Skies Above Sicily

1. Patton's diaries, 11 July 1943, Box 3, Folder 4.
2. Blumenson, *The Patton Papers, 1940-1945,* 282.
3. Chandler, Alfred D. (ed.). *The Papers of Dwight David Eisenhower, The War Years: II* (Baltimore: Johns Hopkins Press), 1255.
4. Patton's diaries, 13 July 1943, Box 3, Folder 2.
5. Investigation of Friendly Fire Incident, n.d., Box 49, Folder 9.

Patton's Old Friend, Paddy

1. Phillips, *The Making of a Professional: Manton S. Eddy, USA,* 5.
2. OV 15, 1.

3. Phillips, *The Making of a Professional: Manton S. Eddy, USA*, 122.
4. GSP to Paddy Flint, 12 June 1944, Box 29, Folder 17.
5. "Keeping Faith: A Tribute to Col. Harry Albert Flint," Box 52, Folder 12; and Phillips, *The Making of a Professional: Manton S. Eddy, USA*, 147.
6. "Keeping Faith," Box 52, Folder 12; GSP to Sallie Flint, 13 July 1944, Box 29, Folder 13; and D'Este, *Patton: A Genius For War*, 741.

Chapter 4: Limbo

1. GSP to BAP, 13 September 1943, 7 October 1943, and 29 December 1943, Box 19, Folders 15 and 17.
2. Patton's diaries, 14–15 December 1943, Box 3, Folder 4.
3. Patton's diaries, 15 December 1943, Box 3, Folder 4.
4. OV 15, 46; GSP to BAP, 13 September 1943, Box 19, Folder 15.
5. Patton's diaries, 21 January 1944, Box 3, Folder 4.
6. Patton's diaries, 4 May 1944, Box 3, Folder 5.
7. OV 16, 39.
8. GSP to BAP, 6 July 1944, Box 12, Folder 3.
9. OV 16, 41; Patton's diaries, 29 October 1943, Box 3, Folder 3.
10. OV 16, 19.
11. OV 16, 46.
12. OV 11, 47; Patton's diaries, 14–15 December 1943, Box 3, Folder 4.
13. OV 16, 49.
14. Blumenson, *The Patton Papers, 1940–1945*, 395–396.
15. OV 16, 52.
16. OV 16, 52; GSP to BAP, 11 January 1944, Box 9, Folder 18.
17. OV 15, 28; Patton's diaries, 21 January 1944, Box 3, Folder 4.
18. OV 15, 2; Patton's diaries, 23 October 1943, Box 3, Folder 3; and 22 January 1944, Box 3, Folder 4.
19. OV 17, 5; Blumenson, *The Patton Papers, 1940–1945*, 411.
20. OV 17, 6; Patton's diaries, 6 May 1944, Box 3, Folder 5.
21. OV 17, 26; GSP to BAP, 6 March 1944, Box 18, Folder 2; and Blumenson, *The Patton Papers, 1940–1945*, 421.
22. OV 17, 17; GSP to BAP, 6 March 1944, Box 18, Folder 2; and Blumenson, *The Patton Papers, 1940–1945*, 482.
23. OV 17, 29; Blumenson, *The Patton Papers, 1940–1945*, 421.
24. OV 17, 17.
25. OV 17, 25; Blumenson, *The Patton Papers, 1940–1945*, 444.
26. OV 17, 26; Patton's diaries, 5 July 1944, Box 3, Folder 6; and Blumenson, *The Patton Papers, 1940–1945*, 473.

Patton Under Fire

1. "Gen. Patton's Brush With Death Revealed," n. d., Box 14, Folder 13.

Chapter 5: France

1. Blumenson, *The Patton Papers, 1940–1945*, 477.
2. GSP to BAP, 26 August 1944, Box 18, Folder 7.
3. Blumenson, *The Patton Papers, 1940–1945*, 488.
4. Blumenson, *The Patton Papers, 1940–1945*, 499.
5. GSP to GM, 5 December 1944, Box 34, Folder 5.
6. Patton's diaries, 13 September 1944, Box 3, Folder 7.
7. GSP to BAP, 4 October 1944, Box 18, Folder 10.
8. Patton's diaries, 8 October 1944, Box 3, Folder 8; and Rickard, *Patton at Bay*, 147.
9. GSP to BAP, 17 October 1944 and 24 October 1944, Box 18, Folder 10.

10. GSP to BAP, 10 November 1944, Box 18, Folder 11.

11. GSP to BAP, 8 July 1944 and 12 July 1944, Box 18, Folder 6; and GSP to BAP, 10 June 1944, Box 12, Folder 2.

12. OV 15, 12; GSP to BAP, 12 July 1944, Box 18, Folder 6; and GSP to BAP, 4 October 1944, Box 18, Folder 10.

13. OV 17, 66; GSP to BAP, 10 July 1944, Box 18, Folder 6.

14. GSP to H.L. Stimpson, 16 August 1944, Box 12, Folder 6.

15. Patton's diaries, 25 July 1944, Box 3, Folder 6.

16. GSP paper on France, "Notes on France," Box 12, Folder 3, George S. Patton Collection, Manuscripts Division, Library of Congress.

17. OV 17, 45.

18. OV 20, 36; Patton's diaries, 12 August 1944, Box 3, Folder 7.

19. OV 20, 1.

20. OV 17, 44; Patton's diaries, 27 August 1944, Box 3, Folder 7.

21. Patton's diaries, 9 September 1944, Box 3, Folder 7.

22. OV 17, 60; GSP to GM, 27 September 1944, Box 34, Folder 5.

23. OV 20, 15.

24. Blumenson, *The Patton Papers, 1940–1945*, 573–574.

25. GSP to BAP, 19 November 1944, Box 18, Folder 11.

26. OV 20, 51; Allen, *Lucky Forward*, 179.

27. GSP to BAP, 16 April 1918, Box 16, Folder 23.

28. MacArthur, *Reminiscences*, 62.

29. Pearl, *Blood-and-Guts Patton*, 9.

30. Blumenson, *The Patton Papers, 1885–1940*, 585.

31. Blumenson, *The Patton Papers, 1885–1940*, 586.

32. Archer, *Front-Line General: Douglas MacArthur*, 57, 184.

33. D'Est, *Patton: Genius for War*, 235, 858.

34. D'Este, *Patton: A Genius for War*, 36.

Meeting MacArthur in World War 1

1. OV 18, 45.

2. OV 20, 5; Patton's diaries, 13 September 1944, Box 3, Folder 7; "Notes on France," 14 September 1944, Box 12, Folder 8; and GSP to GP IV, 17 September 1944, Box 21, Folder 4.

3. OV 17, 56; Patton's diaries, 22 September 1944, Box 3, Folder 7; and GSP to BAP, 21 November 1944, Box 18, Folder 12.

4. OV 20, 25; Patton's diaries, 8 October 1944, Box 3, Folder 8.

5. OV 20, 4; Patton's diaries, 12 October 1944, Box 3, Folder 8.

6. OV 20, 31; Patton's diaries, 16 October 1944, Box 3, Folder 8; and GSP to BAP, 11 October 1944, Box 18, Folder 10.

7. OV 20, 44.

8. OV 20, 41–42.

Patton's Camera Goes Hollywood

1. Pearl, *General Douglas MacArthur*, 56–57.

Chapter 6: The Battle of the Bulge

1. Blumenson, *The Patton Papers, 1940–1945*, 582.

2. Codman, *Drive*, 230.

3. Blumenson, *Patton: The Man Behind the Legend, 1885–1945*, 252.

4. GSP to BAP, 7 January 1945, Box 18, Folder 15.

5. Blumenson, *The Patton Papers, 1940–1945*, 631.

6. Patton's diaries, 26 November 1944, Box 3, Folder 8.

7. Blumenson, *The Patton Papers, 1940–1945*, 635.

8. Patton's diaries, 14 December 1944, Box 3, Folder 9.

9. Patton's diaries, 14 December 1944, Box 3, Folder 9.
10. Patton's diaries, 11 December 1944, Box 3, Folder 9; and GSP to BAP, 26 December 1944, Box 18, Folder 14.
11. OV 18, 36.
12. OV 18, 24.
13. OV 18, 40.
14. Codman, *Drive,* 230.
15. OV 18, 25.
16. Blumenson, *The Patton Papers, 1940–1945,* 609; OV 18, 9; and Patton's diaries, 1 March 1945, Box 3, Folder 10.
17. OV 20, 50.
18. GSP to BAP, 9 January 1945, Box 12, Folder 18.
19. Blumenson, *The Patton Papers, 1940–1945,* 627.

Patton Prepares for the Bulge

1. Patton's diaries, 25 November 1944, Box 3, Folder 8.
2. GSP to BAP, 19 November 1944, Box 11, Folder 12.
3. OV 19, 20.
4. Irzyk, *He Rode Up Front for Patton,* 228–229.
5. Patton's diaries, 12 December 1944, Box 4 , Folder 2.

Chapter 7: Germany

1. GSP to FA, 21 February 1945, Box 14, Folder 19; Patton's diaries, 13 February 1945, Box 3, Folder 10.
2. Patton's diaries, 1 March 1945, Box 3, Folder 10.
3. Codman, *Drive,* 269.
4. Patton's diaries, 20 February 1945, Box 3, Folder 10; and GSP to FA, 21 February 1945, Box 14, Folder 19.
5. Blumenson, *Patton: The Man Behind the Legend, 1885–1945,* 260–261; Baron et. al, *Raid!,* 201.
6. Allen, *Lucky Forward,* 382.
7. GSP to BAP, n. d., Box 13, Folder 7.
8. GSP to BAP, n. d., Box 13, Folder 7.
9. OV 19, 7; Patton's diaries, 20 February 1945, Box 3, Folder 10; and GSP to FA, 21 February 1945, Box 14, Folder 19.
10. OV 19, 7; Patton's diaries, 2 March 1945, Box 3, Folder 10.
11. OV 19, 18; Patton's diaries, 4 March 1945, Box 3, Folder 10.
12. OV 19, 4; Prefer, *Patton's Ghost Corps,* 149 and 187.
13. Patton's diaries, 16 February 1945; and 11 March 1945, Box 3, Folder 10.
13A. Patton's diaries, 22 March 1945, Box 3, Folder 11; and GSP to BAP, 23 March 1945, Box 11, Folder 2.
14. OV 19, 15; Codman, *Drive,* 270.
15. GSP to BAP, 25 March 1945, Box 19, Folder 1; and Patton's diaries, 24 March 1945, Box 3, Folder 4.
16. OV 19, 30.
17. OV 19, 31; Patton diaries 6–9 April 1945, Box 3, Folder 11.
18. OV 19, 54; Patton's diaries, 27 April 1945, Box 3, Folder 12.
19. GSP to BAP, 28 April 1945, Box 13, Folder 6; and GSP to H.L. Stimpson, 1 May 1945, Box 13, Folder 7.
20. GSP to BAP, 28 April 1945, Box 13, Folder 6; and Patton's diaries, 27 April 1945, Box 3, Folder 12.
21. OV 11, 10; Codman, *Drive,* 294.
22. OV 11, 8.
23. OV 11, 8; Codman, *Drive,* 296; GSP to BAP, n. d., Box 13, Folder 7.
24. OV 21, 26; GSP to BAP, 30 April 1945, Box 13, Folder 6.
25. OV 19, 47.
26. OV 19, 51.
27. OV 18, 59; Codman, *Drive,* 294; and GSP to BAP, n. d., Box 13, Folder 7.
28. OV 19, 46; Patton's diaries, 8 May 1945, Box 3, Folder 12.

29. OV 19, 13; GSP to F.P. Graves, 6 April 1945; and 1 May 1945, Box 30, Folder 3.
30. Blumenson, *The Patton Papers, 1940–1945*, 676.

Planes Over Hammelburg

1. Patton's Diaries, 20 March 1943, Box 3, Folder 4.
2. Baron et. al, *Raid!* 10–15.
3. This and all Abe Baum quotes come from an interview by the author with Baum, 18 July 2005.
4. Spires, *Patton's Air Force*, 273.

Chapter 8: Postwar

1. GSP to BAP, 18 May 1945, Box 13, Folder 7.
2. Farago, *The Last Days of Patton*, 78–87.
3. Patton's diaries, 14 October 1945, Box 3, Folder 13.
4. Patton's diaries, 25 November 1945, Box 3, Folder 13.
5. OV 19, 36; Patton's diaries, 12 May 1945, Box 3, Folder 12.
6. Patton's diaries, 24 May 1945, Box 18, Folder 8.
7. Farago, *The Last Days of Patton*, 66.
8. GSP to BAP, 21 July 1945, Box 13, Folder 11; and Blumenson, *The Patton Papers, 1885–1940*, 231.
9. General Patton from Boston, sound recording of Armed Forces Radio broadcast, 7 June 1945, David Goldin Collection, 1932–1952, *Motion Picture, Sound, and Video Records Department, LICON,* National Archives and Records Administration.
10. OV 11, 30.
11. OV 11, 37.
12. OV 11, 34; General Patton from Boston, 7 June 1945, sound recording.
13. General Patton from Boston, 7 June 1945, sound recording.
14. City of Beverly, MA, website, www.beverlyma.gov/Public_Document/MA-Mayor/Index.
15. General Patton from Los Angeles, 9 June 1945, sound recording, David Goldin Collection, *Motion Picture, Sound, and Video Records Department, LICON,* National Archives and Records Administration.
16. OV 11, 46.
17. OV 21, 29; Farago, *The Last Days of Patton*, 87.
18. OV 19, 34; GSP to BAP, 2 September 1945, Box 13, Folder 14.
19. Farago, *The Last Days of Patton*, 216.
20. OV 21, 43.
21. OV 21, 54.

Get Well, General Patton

1. Get-well books, Boxes 37 and 38; and Farago, *The Last Days of Patton*, 226–282.

BIBLIOGRAPHY

Unpublished Sources
The diaries, letters, scrapbooks, and photo albums of Gen. George S. Patton can be found in the George S. Patton collection in the Manuscripts Division of the Library of Congress.

Patton's speeches in the United States in 1945 can be found in the Motion Picture, Sound and Video Records Department at the National Archives and Records Administration. Army Signal Corps photographs can be found the in the Archives' Still Pictures Department.

Interviews
Baum, Maj. Abe, USA (Ret), with author, July 18, 2005
Irzyk, Brig. Gen. Albin, USA (Ret.), with author, May 10, 2005.
Kerwin, Gen. Walter T., USA (Ret), with author, May 5, 2005.

Published Sources
Allen, Col. Robert S. *Lucky Forward: The History of Patton's Third Army.* New York: The Vanguard Press, 1947.

Archer, Jules. *Front-line General: Douglas MacArthur.* New York: Julian Messner, 1963.

Atkinson, Rick. *An Army at Dawn: War in North Africa, 1942–1943.* New York: Henry Holt, 2002.

Baron, Richard, Maj. Abe Baum and Richard Goldhurst. *Raid! The Untold Story of Patton's Secret Mission.* New York: Dell, 1981.

Blumenson, Martin. *The Duel for France, 1944: The Men and Battles that Changed the Fate of Europe.* Cambridge, MA: Da Capo Press, 1963.

___. *Patton: The Man Behind the Legend, 1885–1945.* New York: William Morrow, 1985.

___. *The Patton Papers, 1885–1940.* Boston: Houghton Mifflin, 1972.

___. *The Patton Papers, 1940–1945.* Boston: Houghton Mifflin, 1974.

Codman, Charles R. *Drive.* Boston: Little, Brown. 1957.

D'Este, Carlo. *Patton: A Genius for War.* New York: HarperCollins, 1995.

Farago, Ladislas. *The Last Days of Patton.* New York: Berkley Books, 1984.

___. *Patton: Ordeal and Triumph.* New York: Ivan Obolensky, 1964.

Forty, George. *The Armies of George S. Patton.* London: Arms and Armour Press, 1996.

Irzyk, Albin F. *He Rode Up Front for Patton.* Raleigh, NC: Portland Press, 1996.

MacArthur, Douglas. *Reminiscences.* New York: McGraw-Hill, 1964.

MacDonald, Charles B. *A Time for Trumpets: The Untold Story of the Battle of the Bulge.* New York: William Morrow, 1985.

Mercer, Derrik, ed. *Chronicle of the World.* New York: DK Publishing, 1996.

Patton, George S., Jr. *War as I Knew It.* New York: Bantam Books, 1979.

Patton, Robert H. *The Pattons: A Personal History of an American Family.* New York: Crown Publishers, 1994.

Pearl, Jack. *Blood and Guts Patton: The Swashbuckling Life Story of America's Most Daring and Controversial General.* Derby, CO: Monarch Books, 1961.

___. *General Douglas MacArthur.* Derby, CO: Monarch Books, 1961.

Phillips, Henry Gerard. *The Making of a Professional: Manton S. Eddy, USA.* Westport, CT: Greenwood Press, 2000.

Polmar, Norman and Thomas B. Allen. *World War II: America at War 1941–1945.* New York: Random House, 1991.

Prefer, Nathan. *Patton's Ghost Corps: Cracking the Siegfried Line.* New York: Presidio Press, 1997.

Rickard, John Nelson. *Patton at Bay: The Lorraine Campaign, September to December, 1944.* Westport, CT: Praeger, 1999.

Spires, David N. *Patton's Air Force: Forging a Legendary Air-Ground Team.* Washington: Smithsonian Institution Press, 2002.

Weigley, Russell. *Eisenhower's Lieutenants: The Campaign of France and Germany, 1944-1945.* Bloomington: Indiana University Press, 1990.

INDEX

ABOUT THE AUTHOR

KEVIN M. HYMEL is the Associate Editor for *ARMY* Magazine where he writes the news stories and reviews books. As the Research Director for Sovereign Media, he researches photos and artwork to accompany military history stories for *WWII History* and *Military Heritage* magazines. He also contributes stories, photo essays and sidebars to the magazines. Mr. Hymel has worked as a World War II tour guide for Ambrose Tours and as a researcher for the Army Historical Foundation. He graduated from LaSalle University with a BA in American History and earned a master's degree in American History from Villanova University. He lives in Arlington, Virginia.